Comprehensive Guide

Global Governance Practices

John Roxburgh

Table of Contents

Chapter 1: Introduction

I am honored to present this comprehensive guide on designing and implementing effective governance practices. Drawing on my extensive experience in governance, risk, and compliance, I have developed this guide to provide professionals like you with the knowledge and tools necessary to navigate the complex landscape of governance and drive organizational success.

About the Author

As the author of this guide and Managing Director of Governance Solutions Australia, John Roxburgh brings over 25 years of experience in Enterprise Technology and Corporate Governance. Throughout his distinguished career, John has been dedicated to achieving operational excellence through the implementation of global best practices and effective frameworks that target the optimization of business value.

John's extensive expertise lies in governance frameworks, enabling the successful implementation of global standards and the application of best practices in governance, risk, and compliance (GRC) management. His integrated GRC solutions have consistently delivered on strategic objectives, ensuring timely and budget-conscious outcomes while maintaining regulatory compliance and effectively managing risks across both Technology and Business operations.

Working with organizations of all sizes, John has witnessed firsthand the transformative impact of effective governance practices. His broad range of knowledge extends beyond governance to encompass risk management, compliance, and operations. This breadth of understanding allows John to provide a comprehensive and interconnected perspective on the disciplines covered within this guide.

Throughout this guide, John leverages his wealth of experience and insights to equip readers with practical knowledge and actionable guidance in the realm of governance best practices. His expertise and dedication to excellence make him a trusted authority in the field, and readers can rely on his expertise to navigate the complexities of governance, risk management, and compliance.

Purpose of the Guide

The objective of this guide is to provide you with a comprehensive and in-depth understanding of governance, highlighting its significance in contemporary business environments. Through the exploration of key topics and principles, this guide aims to equip you with practical insights and best practices that can be applied to enhance governance within your organization.

The information presented in this guide is grounded in global best practices and established governance standards. It has been meticulously crafted to ensure accessibility for GRC professionals and business leaders alike, allowing for easy extraction of relevant information that can be effectively incorporated into presentations and other materials. By leveraging the insights and recommendations provided in this guide, you will be well-equipped to articulate the importance and effectiveness of GRC within your organization.

With a focus on clarity, depth, and professionalism, this guide serves as a valuable resource for individuals seeking to strengthen governance practices, drive organizational success, and foster a culture of accountability and integrity.

Disclaimer and Licensing Information

While this guide strives to provide accurate and up-to-date information, it is important to note that governance, risk, and compliance landscapes are constantly evolving. Therefore, it is essential to consult with relevant experts and refer to the latest industry standards and regulations to ensure the applicability of the information presented. This guide is intended for informational purposes only and should not substitute professional advice or legal counsel.

Copyright Notice

Chapter 2: Understanding Governance

2.1 Definition and Evolution of Governance

Governance, in its broadest sense, refers to the framework of rules, processes, and structures that guide and control an organization's actions and behaviours. It encompasses decision-making, accountability, risk management, compliance, and ethical practices. The concept of governance has evolved significantly over time, adapting to the changing business landscape, societal expectations, and the increasing complexity of organizations.

Historically, governance can be traced back to ancient civilizations, where early forms of governance were established to manage social, economic, and political systems. As societies progressed, governance frameworks emerged to address the challenges of growing organizations and the need for effective leadership and control.

2.2 History and Development of Governance Standards and Frameworks

To promote consistent and effective governance practices, several standards and frameworks have been developed and refined over time. These standards provide organizations with guidance and best practices to ensure their governance processes align with industry norms and expectations. Let's explore some key governance standards that have emerged:

- **ISO 38500:** Focuses on corporate governance of IT, providing guidance on the role of IT in organizational governance.

- **ISO 31000:** Provides principles and guidelines for effective risk management, helping organizations identify, assess, and mitigate risks.

- **ISO 9001:** Sets out criteria for implementing a quality management system to enhance customer satisfaction and overall performance.

- **ISO 23635:** Specifically applicable to distributed ledger technology (DLT), this standard addresses governance considerations and risk management in blockchain environments.

- **ISO 37301:** Provides guidelines for establishing an effective compliance management system, ensuring adherence to laws, regulations, and ethical practices.

- **ISO 37000:** Focuses on organizational change management, providing guidance on managing and implementing change initiatives within a governance framework.
- **COBIT 2019:** A framework for IT governance and management, guiding organizations in aligning IT strategies with business objectives.

- **CMMI:** The Capability Maturity Model Integration is a framework for process improvement and governance, helping organizations enhance their capability and maturity in various domains.

- **OECD Principles of Corporate Governance:** Provides recommendations for good governance practices, focusing on transparency, accountability, and equitable treatment of shareholders.

- **COSO Framework:** Provides guidance on internal control, risk management, and fraud prevention.

- **IIA Standards**: Includes the International Professional Practices Framework (IPPF) for internal auditing, risk management, and governance processes.

- **NIST Cybersecurity Framework:** Provides guidelines and best practices for managing and mitigating cybersecurity risks.

- **King IV Report:** Provides principles and practices for effective governance, with an emphasis on ethical leadership, stakeholder inclusivity, and integrated reporting.

These standards continue to evolve to address emerging challenges and incorporate industry best practices, reflecting the ongoing development of governance principles and frameworks.

2.3 Key Principles and Objectives of Governance

Governance is guided by a set of key principles and objectives that shape its implementation. While the specific principles may vary across organizations and frameworks, the following principles are commonly embraced:

- **Accountability:** Governance promotes clear lines of responsibility, ensuring individuals and entities are answerable for their actions, decisions, and performance. It establishes mechanisms to track and evaluate accountability, such as setting performance metrics, conducting regular performance assessments, and holding individuals and entities responsible for meeting their obligations. Accountability fosters a culture of ownership, ensuring that all stakeholders are aware of their roles and responsibilities and are committed to fulfilling them effectively.

- **Transparency:** Governance emphasizes openness and accessibility of information, enabling stakeholders to make informed decisions and understand how decisions are made. It involves sharing relevant information with stakeholders in a timely and accurate manner, providing them with insight into the organization's operations, financial performance, decision-making processes, and potential risks. Transparent governance practices build trust, enhance stakeholder confidence, and promote effective engagement and participation.

- **Integrity:** Governance upholds ethical behaviour, honesty, and fairness in all aspects of organizational operations, fostering trust among stakeholders. It involves setting and promoting high ethical standards, establishing codes of conduct, and ensuring compliance with legal and regulatory requirements. Integrity-driven governance practices discourage conflicts of interest, corruption, and unethical behaviours, creating a culture of trust and integrity within the organization.

- **Compliance:** Governance ensures adherence to laws, regulations, and industry standards, mitigating legal and reputational risks. It involves establishing internal controls, policies, and procedures to ensure compliance and monitoring mechanisms to identify and address compliance gaps. Compliance-focused governance practices enable organizations to operate within the boundaries of the law, protect their reputation, and maintain the trust of stakeholders.

- **Risk management:** Governance incorporates robust risk management practices, enabling organizations to identify, assess, and address potential risks to achieve objectives. It involves establishing risk management frameworks and processes to identify and analyse risks, develop risk mitigation strategies, and monitor risk exposure. Effective risk management in governance ensures that organizations can proactively identify and respond to risks, safeguarding their assets, reputation, and long-term sustainability.

- **Strategic alignment:** Governance aligns organizational activities and decision-making with strategic objectives, ensuring consistent progress towards desired outcomes. It involves establishing strategic planning processes, setting clear goals and objectives, and aligning resources and actions to achieve them. Strategic alignment in governance ensures that all decisions and actions are guided by the organization's mission, vision, and strategic priorities, fostering organizational coherence and effectiveness.

- **Stakeholder focus:** Governance considers the interests and expectations of stakeholders, maintaining positive relationships and delivering value to all relevant parties. It involves engaging with stakeholders, understanding their needs and concerns, and incorporating their perspectives into decision-making processes. Stakeholder-focused governance practices promote effective communication, collaboration, and mutual understanding, leading to better decision-making and increased stakeholder satisfaction.

- By adhering to these principles, organizations can establish a solid foundation for sustainable success. Effective governance practices that embody accountability, transparency, integrity, compliance, risk management, strategic alignment, and stakeholder focus contribute to organizational resilience, ethical conduct, and long-term value creation.

Chapter 3: Governance Applicability for Every Organization

3.1 Importance of Governance in Organizations of All Sizes

Governance is not limited to large corporations; it is equally crucial for organizations of all sizes. Regardless of their scale, organizations must establish effective governance practices to ensure operational efficiency, risk management, and stakeholder satisfaction. Whether it is a small business, a non-profit organization, or a government entity, the principles of good governance apply universally.

Even small businesses can benefit significantly from governance by establishing clear roles and responsibilities, implementing financial controls, and ensuring transparent decision-making. Non-profit organizations must adhere to governance principles to build donor trust, demonstrate accountability, and fulfill their mission effectively. Government entities require robust governance frameworks to ensure transparency, fairness, and efficient service delivery.

3.2 Tailoring Governance Practices to Suit Different Organizational Needs

While the principles of governance remain consistent, the implementation of governance practices must be tailored to suit the specific needs and characteristics of different organizations. Factors to consider when designing governance frameworks include:

- **Organizational size and complexity:** Larger organizations often require more formal and elaborate governance structures to manage diverse operations and stakeholders. For example, they may establish board committees, such as audit committees or risk management committees, to oversee specific areas. On the other hand, smaller organizations can adopt simpler frameworks that align with their size and resources, such as having a small board of directors with clear decision-making processes.

- **Industry and sector-specific requirements:** Different industries may have unique regulatory requirements or specific governance expectations. For instance, financial institutions may need to comply with strict regulations related to capital requirements and risk management. Healthcare organizations may have to adhere to privacy and data security standards. Governance practices should align with these industry-specific standards to ensure compliance and effective risk management. For example, an IT company may establish an IT governance framework that addresses cybersecurity and data protection.

- **Organizational culture and values:** Governance practices should be designed to align with the organization's culture and values. For instance, a company that values innovation and agility may incorporate governance practices that encourage experimentation and quick decision-making. Embedding governance within the organizational DNA ensures that it becomes an integral part of day-to-day operations and decision-making processes. For example, an organization committed to sustainability may include environmental and social responsibility considerations in its governance practices.

- **Stakeholder expectations:** Organizations should consider the needs and expectations of their stakeholders when designing governance frameworks. Stakeholder engagement and feedback play a vital role in shaping effective governance practices. For example, a consumer goods company may establish mechanisms for gathering feedback from customers and incorporating it into decision-making processes. Non-profit organizations may engage with their beneficiaries to ensure that governance practices align with their needs and priorities.

By tailoring governance practices to suit organizational needs, organizations can strike a balance between structure and flexibility, ensuring that governance processes support their specific goals and objectives. This approach allows organizations to maximize the benefits of governance while addressing the unique challenges and opportunities they face.

Effective governance enhances organizational performance, promotes ethical conduct, and fosters long-term sustainability. Regardless of the organization's size or sector, implementing appropriate governance practices is essential for achieving success and maintaining stakeholder trust.

Chapter 4: Consequences of Poor Governance

4.1 Impact of Poor Governance on Business Performance

Poor governance can have severe consequences for organizational performance and sustainability. When governance practices fail to provide adequate oversight, control, and transparency, the following negative outcomes may arise:

- **Inefficient decision-making:** Without proper governance structures, decision-making processes can become fragmented, leading to delays, confusion, and suboptimal outcomes.

- **Lack of accountability:** Poor governance may result in a lack of clarity regarding roles and responsibilities, leading to a culture of finger-pointing and a failure to address performance issues.

- **Mismanagement of resources:** Ineffective governance can result in the misallocation of resources, inefficient use of funds, and failure to capitalize on growth opportunities.

- **Inadequate risk management:** Without robust governance frameworks, organizations may struggle to identify, assess, and mitigate risks effectively, exposing them to potential financial and reputational harm.

Insufficient governance practices can erode trust and confidence among stakeholders, including customers, investors, employees, and regulators, damaging relationships, and impacting long-term success.

4.2 Legal and Regulatory Consequences of Ineffective Governance

In addition to the negative impact on business performance, poor governance can lead to legal and regulatory challenges. Non-compliance with laws, regulations, and industry standards can result in penalties, fines, litigation, and reputational damage. Regulatory bodies and industry watchdogs closely scrutinize organizations' governance practices to ensure compliance and protect the interests of stakeholders.

Examples of legal and regulatory consequences include:

- **Breach of fiduciary duty:** Failure to act in the best interest of stakeholders, such as shareholders, can result in legal action and claims of breach of fiduciary duty.

- **Violation of data privacy regulations:** Inadequate governance practices regarding data protection can lead to data breaches, violating privacy regulations and triggering legal repercussions.
- **Non-compliance with financial reporting requirements:** Inaccurate or misleading financial reporting due to weak governance controls can result in regulatory investigations, fines, and reputational damage.

- **Anti-corruption and bribery violations:** Organizations that lack effective governance measures to prevent corrupt practices may face legal action and regulatory penalties.

To mitigate legal and regulatory risks, organizations must establish robust governance practices that ensure compliance with relevant laws and regulations.

4.3 Reputational Risks and Stakeholder Confidence

Effective governance is closely linked to an organization's reputation and stakeholder confidence. A strong reputation built on transparent, ethical, and responsible governance practices can enhance stakeholder trust and attract customers, investors, and top talent. Conversely, poor governance practices can erode trust, damage reputation, and lead to significant financial and operational setbacks.

Examples of reputational risks stemming from poor governance include:

- **Corporate scandals and misconduct:** High-profile cases of corporate misconduct, such as fraud, unethical behaviour, or breaches of trust, can severely tarnish an organization's reputation and erode stakeholder confidence.

- **Data breaches and security incidents:** Inadequate governance practices regarding data security can result in data breaches, leading to reputational damage and a loss of customer trust.

- **Environmental and social responsibility failures:** Organizations that fail to integrate environmental and social considerations into their governance practices may face public backlash and damage their reputation among socially conscious stakeholders.

- **Non-compliance with ethical standards:** Failure to adhere to ethical standards and values, such as diversity and inclusion, fair labour practices, and human rights, can harm an organization's reputation and negatively impact stakeholder perception.

4.4 Financial Implications of Inadequate Governance

In addition to the legal, regulatory, and reputational risks, poor governance can have significant financial implications for organizations. Inefficient use of resources, increased operational costs, and loss of revenue can erode profitability and hinder long-term sustainability.

Financial consequences of inadequate governance may include:

- **Loss of investor confidence:** Weak governance practices can erode investor confidence in an organization. Investors are more likely to invest in companies that have strong governance structures and transparent decision-making processes. When governance is lacking, potential investors may perceive higher risks associated with the organization's operations and management, leading them to avoid investing or providing financial support. Existing investors may also withdraw their support, causing a decline in capital infusion. The loss of investor confidence restricts the organization's ability to raise funds, limiting its growth opportunities and potentially impacting its financial stability.

- **Increased borrowing costs:** Organizations with poor governance may face higher borrowing costs when seeking external financing. Lenders assess the risk profile of a company before extending credit. Inadequate oversight and control mechanisms signal higher risk, as they can lead to financial mismanagement, fraudulent activities, or ineffective decision-making. Consequently, lenders may demand higher interest rates or impose stricter borrowing terms to compensate for the perceived risk. These increased borrowing costs can put additional strain on the organization's finances, reducing its profitability and financial flexibility.

- **Inefficient resource allocation:** Ineffective governance can result in the misallocation of financial resources within an organization. Poorly defined decision-making processes, lack of transparency, or conflicts of interest can lead to suboptimal allocation of funds. This misallocation can manifest in various ways, such as investing in non-profitable ventures, excessive spending on unnecessary activities, or failing to allocate resources to critical areas. Inefficient resource allocation hampers the organization's ability to maximize its financial returns, seize growth opportunities, and operate at optimal efficiency, ultimately reducing profitability.

- **Internal fraud and embezzlement:** Weak governance controls increase the risk of internal fraud, embezzlement, and financial mismanagement within an organization. Inadequate oversight, lax internal controls, and a lack of checks and balances create an environment conducive to fraudulent activities. This can involve employees misappropriating funds, manipulating financial records, or engaging in other illicit practices. Internal fraud and embezzlement can result in significant financial losses for the organization, impacting its bottom line and damaging its reputation. Detecting and rectifying such fraudulent activities can be costly and time-consuming, further straining the organization's financial resources.

Understanding these potential financial consequences highlights the importance of implementing robust governance practices. By establishing effective oversight mechanisms, transparent decision-making processes, and strong internal controls, organizations can mitigate these risks, enhance financial stability, and ensure long-term success.

Chapter 5: ISO 38500: Corporate Governance of IT

5.1 Overview of ISO 38500 Standard

ISO 38500 provides guidance for governing the management of IT within an organization. It focuses on the role of the governing body in setting strategic direction, evaluating performance, and ensuring that IT investments align with business objectives. The standard emphasizes the need for effective decision-making, accountability, and transparency in IT governance.

5.2 Key Principles and Framework Components

The ISO 38500 standard is built upon a set of key principles that organizations should adhere to when governing IT. These principles include:

- **Responsibility:** The governing body of an organization should take overall responsibility for IT governance. This includes ensuring that IT initiatives align with organizational goals and objectives, and that they add value to the organization. The governing body should oversee the strategic direction of IT, set policies, and allocate necessary resources for effective IT governance.

- **Strategy:** IT should be managed as an integral part of the organization's overall strategy. This principle emphasizes the need for aligning IT initiatives with the broader business objectives. By incorporating IT into the strategic planning process, organizations can leverage technology to enable and enhance their ability to achieve business goals, drive innovation, and gain a competitive advantage.

- **Acquisition:** IT investments and services should be acquired in a planned and structured manner. This principle highlights the importance of considering the costs, risks, and benefits associated with IT investments. Organizations should adopt a systematic approach to assess and select IT solutions, considering factors such as functionality, compatibility, security, and long-term sustainability. This ensures that IT investments are in line with the organization's objectives and deliver optimal value.

- **Performance:** Regular evaluation and monitoring of IT performance are essential to ensure its effectiveness and contribution to organizational goals. This principle emphasizes the need for establishing performance metrics and monitoring mechanisms to assess the performance of IT initiatives, systems, and processes. By evaluating IT performance, organizations can identify areas for improvement, make informed decisions regarding resource allocation, and ensure that IT activities align with strategic objectives.

- **Conformance:** IT practices should conform to relevant laws, regulations, and internal policies, while also considering ethical considerations. This principle emphasizes the need for organizations to comply with legal and regulatory requirements governing IT activities, such as data protection, privacy, and intellectual property rights. Additionally, organizations should establish internal policies and standards that guide the ethical conduct of IT professionals and promote responsible and sustainable IT practices.

- **Human behaviour:** The governance of IT should consider human behaviour, fostering a culture of responsibility, accountability, and ethical conduct. This principle recognizes that the success of IT governance relies not only on processes and technologies but also on the behaviour and attitudes of individuals involved. Organizations should promote a culture that encourages ethical conduct, responsible decision-making, and effective communication to ensure the successful implementation of IT governance practices.

Framework Components of ISO 38500 include:

- **Governance Framework:** The governance framework provides the overall structure and guidelines for IT governance within an organization. It includes the definition of roles, responsibilities, and decision-making processes related to IT governance. The framework outlines the key elements and practices that enable effective IT governance and ensures alignment with organizational objectives.

- **Governance Process:** The governance process refers to the activities and steps involved in managing and overseeing IT governance. It includes strategic planning, risk management, performance evaluation, resource allocation, and decision-making processes. The governance process enables organizations to establish a systematic approach to managing IT, ensuring that IT initiatives are aligned with business goals and effectively contribute to organizational success.

- **Governance Enablers:** Governance enablers encompass the tools, resources, and mechanisms that support the implementation of IT governance practices. These enablers may include policies, guidelines, frameworks, IT infrastructure, human resources, and training programs. They provide organizations with the necessary resources and capabilities to implement and sustain effective IT governance practices as defined by the ISO 38500 standard.

By adhering to the key principles and implementing the framework components outlined in ISO 38500, organizations can establish a robust IT governance framework that aligns IT with business objectives, promotes accountability and transparency, and ensures the effective management of IT resources.

5.3 Integrating ISO 38500 with Other Governance Standards and Practices

ISO 38500 can be integrated with other governance standards and practices to create a comprehensive governance framework. For example, it can be aligned with ISO 9001 for quality management, ISO 31000 for risk management, or COBIT for IT governance and management.

Integration of ISO 38500 with other standards allows organizations to leverage synergies and ensure consistency in governance practices across different domains. It enables a holistic approach to governance, where IT governance is aligned with overall organizational governance objectives.

Chapter 6: ISO 31000: Risk Management

6.1 Introduction to ISO 31000 Standard

ISO 31000 provides guidelines for establishing, implementing, and continually improving risk management processes within an organization. The standard promotes a systematic and proactive approach to risk management, helping organizations identify, assess, treat, and monitor risks effectively.

6.2 Risk Management Process and Framework

ISO 31000 outlines a risk management process consisting of several key steps:

- **Establishing the context:** This step involves understanding the organizational context within which risk management will be performed. It includes identifying the organization's objectives, stakeholders, and the internal and external factors that may influence the risk management process. By establishing the context, organizations can ensure that risk management efforts are aligned with their strategic goals and consider relevant factors that may impact the identification and treatment of risks.

- **Risk assessment:** Risk assessment is the process of identifying and analysing risks. It involves identifying potential risks that may hinder the achievement of objectives and assessing their potential impacts. This step includes evaluating the likelihood of risks occurring and estimating their potential consequences. Risk assessment techniques, such as risk registers, risk matrices, or qualitative and quantitative analysis methods, can be used to assess risks effectively.

- **Risk treatment:** Once risks are identified and assessed, organizations need to develop and implement risk treatment plans. Risk treatment involves selecting and implementing appropriate strategies to mitigate, avoid, transfer, or accept risks. It may involve implementing control measures, developing contingency plans, transferring risk through insurance or contracts, or modifying business processes. The goal is to reduce the likelihood or impact of risks to an acceptable level and enhance the organization's ability to achieve its objectives.

- **Risk monitoring and review:** Risk management is an ongoing process, and regular monitoring and review are essential to ensure its effectiveness. Organizations should establish mechanisms to monitor risks and the effectiveness of risk treatment plans. This includes tracking changes in the risk landscape, reviewing the performance of implemented controls, and identifying emerging risks. Regular reviews enable organizations to make necessary adjustments to their risk management strategies and ensure their continued relevance and effectiveness.

- **Communication and consultation:** Effective communication and consultation with stakeholders are crucial in risk management. Organizations should establish clear channels of communication to share information about risks, risk management strategies, and progress in risk treatment. This includes engaging stakeholders and seeking their input, feedback, and support. Effective communication and consultation foster a shared understanding of risks and risk management across the organization, promote risk awareness, and enhance stakeholder engagement and support.

- **Documentation and reporting:** Documentation and reporting are important aspects of the risk management process. Organizations should document their risk management processes, including the identification, assessment, treatment, and monitoring of risks. This documentation helps ensure consistency, transparency, and accountability in risk management practices. Additionally, organizations should provide timely reports to stakeholders, including senior management and the board, to keep them informed about the organization's risk profile, progress in risk treatment, and any significant changes or emerging risks.

By following the risk management process outlined in ISO 31000, organizations can systematically identify, assess, treat, monitor, and communicate risks. This proactive approach helps organizations better understand their risk landscape, make informed decisions, allocate resources effectively, and enhance their ability to achieve objectives while managing uncertainties.

6.3 Linking Risk Management with Governance and Compliance

Effective risk management is closely linked to governance and compliance. Organizations with robust risk management processes can identify and assess risks that may impact their strategic objectives and take appropriate measures to mitigate or avoid those risks. This integration ensures that risk management aligns with the organization's overall governance framework and compliance requirements.

By incorporating risk management practices into their governance processes, organizations can make informed decisions, allocate resources effectively, and address potential risks that may hinder the achievement of their objectives. Risk management also helps organizations comply with legal and regulatory requirements by identifying and addressing compliance risks.

6.4 Best Practices for Effective Risk Management

To enhance the effectiveness of risk management, organizations can consider the following best practices:

- **Establish a risk management policy:** Developing a formal risk management policy demonstrates the organization's commitment to managing risks effectively. The policy should outline the organization's objectives, approach to risk management, roles and responsibilities, and the overall framework for managing risks. By having a clear policy in place, organizations provide guidance and direction for their employees and stakeholders, ensuring a consistent and coordinated approach to risk management.

- **Involve stakeholders:** Engaging key stakeholders in the risk management process is crucial for obtaining diverse perspectives, expertise, and support. Stakeholders can include senior management, board members, employees, customers, suppliers, and regulatory authorities. Involving stakeholders promotes a sense of ownership and fosters a collaborative approach to risk management. By including stakeholders in risk assessments, decision-making processes, and communication efforts, organizations gain valuable insights and build stakeholder confidence.

- **Integrate risk management into decision-making:** Embedding risk assessment and evaluation into the organization's decision-making processes ensures that risks are considered when making strategic, operational, and project-related decisions. Risk management should be integrated at all levels of the organization, from top-level strategic decisions to day-to-day operational choices. By incorporating risk analysis into decision-making, organizations can make informed choices, balance risks and rewards, and align their risk tolerance with their strategic objectives.

- **Regularly review and update risk assessments:** Risk assessments should be dynamic and responsive to changes in the organization's operating environment. Regularly reviewing and updating risk assessments ensures that risks remain current and reflective of the organization's evolving context. This includes monitoring emerging risks, evaluating the effectiveness of risk treatment measures, and adjusting risk priorities as needed. By keeping risk assessments up to date, organizations can identify new risks, modify mitigation strategies, and maintain an accurate understanding of their risk landscape.

- **Provide adequate resources:** Allocating sufficient resources is essential for effective risk management. This includes assigning skilled personnel who possess risk management expertise and knowledge to drive the risk management process. Adequate resources also encompass providing appropriate tools, technologies, and systems to support risk identification, assessment, and reporting. By investing in resources for risk management, organizations demonstrate their commitment to the process and enable efficient and accurate risk analysis and decision-making.

- **Foster a risk-aware culture:** Promoting a risk-aware culture is vital for creating an environment where risk management is valued and practiced throughout the organization. This involves instilling a sense of responsibility and accountability for risk management at all levels. Encouraging open communication, reporting of near-misses or potential risks, and proactive risk identification helps build a culture where risks are identified early, and appropriate actions are taken. Training programs and awareness campaigns can further promote risk awareness and the importance of individual and collective risk management efforts.

6.5 Benefits of ISO 31000 Implementation

Implementing ISO 31000 and adopting a systematic approach to risk management offers several benefits to organizations:

- **Enhanced risk awareness:** As per the best practice, ISO 31000 helps organizations develop a better understanding of risks and their potential impact on objectives. By following the standard's principles and practices, organizations can identify and assess risks systematically, enabling proactive risk mitigation and better decision-making.

- **Improved decision-making:** Effective risk management, as guided by ISO 31000, facilitates informed decision-making. Organizations gain a comprehensive view of risks, their likelihood, and consequences, enabling them to make decisions that are based on a thorough understanding of potential risks and their potential impacts on objectives.

- **Increased organizational resilience:** By identifying and managing risks, organizations improve their ability to respond to disruptions, mitigate potential losses, and maintain business continuity. Effective risk management enhances the organization's resilience and its capacity to adapt to changing circumstances, protecting its assets, reputation, and long-term sustainability.

- **Stakeholder confidence:** Demonstrating adherence to ISO 31000 principles and implementing robust risk management practices enhances stakeholder confidence, trust, and satisfaction. Stakeholders, including customers, investors, regulators, and business partners, have greater assurance that risks are being managed effectively and that the organization is committed to identifying and addressing potential risks.

- **Compliance with regulations and standards:** ISO 31000 helps organizations meet regulatory requirements and align with industry best practices related to risk management. By implementing the standard, organizations can demonstrate their commitment to effective risk management, which may be required or expected by regulatory authorities, industry bodies, or other stakeholders.

By implementing ISO 31000 and adopting a systematic approach to risk management, organizations can establish a solid foundation for managing risks effectively. This contributes to improved organizational performance, stakeholder satisfaction, and long-term sustainability, as risks are identified, evaluated, and managed in a structured and proactive manner.

Chapter 7: ISO 9001: Quality Management

7.1 Understanding ISO 9001 Standard

ISO 9001 is an internationally recognized standard for quality management systems (QMS). It provides a framework for organizations to establish processes that ensure consistent delivery of products and services that meet customer requirements and enhance customer satisfaction.

7.2 Quality Management Principles and Framework

ISO 9001 is based on a set of quality management principles that guide organizations in achieving excellence in their QMS. These principles include customer focus, leadership, involvement of people, process approach, systematic approach to management, continual improvement, fact-based decision making, and mutually beneficial supplier relationships.

The ISO 9001 framework consists of several key components:

- **Context of the organization:** Organizations need to identify and understand the internal and external factors that impact their quality management system (QMS). This includes considering the needs and expectations of interested parties such as customers, employees, suppliers, regulators, and the community. By understanding the organization's context, organizations can effectively define the scope of their QMS and ensure that it aligns with their strategic objectives and stakeholder requirements.

- **Leadership:** Top management plays a crucial role in establishing and maintaining a successful QMS. They should demonstrate leadership and commitment to quality by defining and communicating the organization's quality policy and objectives. Top management should also ensure that the QMS is integrated into the organization's overall business processes, promote a culture of quality throughout the organization, and allocate necessary resources to support the QMS implementation.

- **Planning:** Planning is essential for effective quality management. Organizations should develop plans that address risks and opportunities related to their QMS. This includes identifying potential risks and taking actions to prevent or mitigate them, as well as identifying opportunities for improvement and leveraging them to enhance the QMS. Additionally, organizations should set quality objectives that are measurable, achievable, and aligned with their overall strategic goals.

- **Support:** Adequate support is necessary to establish and maintain an effective QMS. This includes providing the necessary resources, such as infrastructure, technology, and competent personnel, to support the implementation and operation of the QMS. Organizations should also ensure that documented information, including policies, procedures, work instructions, and records, is readily available to support the effective functioning of the QMS.

- **Operation:** The operation component covers the execution of processes to deliver products and services that meet customer requirements. This includes various activities such as planning, design, purchasing, production, and service delivery. Organizations should establish and control these processes to ensure that products and services consistently meet quality standards and customer expectations. This component emphasizes the importance of systematically managing processes and ensuring that they are properly documented, communicated, and executed.

- **Performance evaluation:** Continuous monitoring, measurement, analysis, and evaluation of the QMS are necessary to ensure its effectiveness. This includes measuring customer satisfaction, evaluating process performance, monitoring product conformity, and conducting internal audits. By assessing performance indicators, organizations can identify areas for improvement, detect nonconformities, and take appropriate corrective and preventive actions.

- **Improvement:** Continual improvement is a core principle of ISO 9001. Organizations should identify opportunities for improvement in their QMS and take actions to enhance its effectiveness and efficiency. This includes analysing data, conducting root cause analysis, implementing corrective actions to address nonconformities, and implementing preventive measures to avoid potential issues. By continually striving for improvement, organizations can enhance customer satisfaction, optimize processes, and drive overall business performance.

By following the ISO 9001 quality management framework, organizations can establish a systematic approach to quality management, ensuring that processes are well-planned, resources are effectively utilized, performance is evaluated, and opportunities for improvement are identified and acted upon. This leads to enhanced customer satisfaction, improved product, and service quality, and increased overall organizational performance.

7.3 Integrating Quality Management with Governance and Risk Practices

Effective quality management is an essential component of good governance and risk management. By implementing ISO 9001, organizations establish processes that help ensure the quality of products and services, which in turn contributes to customer satisfaction, stakeholder confidence, and compliance with regulatory requirements.

Integrating quality management with governance and risk practices enables organizations to make informed decisions based on reliable data and information. It helps them identify and address quality-related risks, ensure compliance with quality standards, and continuously improve their processes and performance.

7.4 Benefits of ISO 9001 Certification for Organizations

ISO 9001 certification provides several benefits to organizations, including:

- **Enhanced customer satisfaction:** Implementing ISO 9001 helps organizations improve their ability to meet customer requirements and deliver consistent quality. The standard emphasizes customer focus, ensuring that customer needs and expectations are understood, and processes are in place to address them effectively. By enhancing customer satisfaction, organizations can build stronger customer relationships, increase customer loyalty, and potentially attract new customers through positive word-of-mouth.

- **Increased operational efficiency:** ISO 9001 promotes the adoption of efficient processes, waste reduction, and streamlined operations. Organizations are encouraged to identify and eliminate non-value-added activities, reduce redundancies, and optimize resource allocation. By improving operational efficiency, organizations can enhance productivity, reduce costs, and improve overall business performance. Efficient processes also lead to faster response times, shorter lead times, and improved delivery performance, further enhancing customer satisfaction.

- **Improved stakeholder confidence:** ISO 9001 certification demonstrates an organization's commitment to quality management and adherence to internationally recognized standards. The certification provides assurance to stakeholders, including customers, suppliers, investors, and regulatory authorities, that the organization has implemented robust quality management practices. This improves stakeholder confidence, builds trust in the organization's capabilities, and enhances its reputation in the marketplace.

- **Competitive advantage:** ISO 9001 certification is globally recognized and respected. Attaining certification can provide organizations with a competitive advantage, especially when competing for contracts or seeking entry into new markets. ISO 9001 certification is often a requirement for participation in public tenders or supplier selection processes. Certification gives organizations a differentiated positioning, demonstrating their commitment to quality and providing a clear advantage over non-certified competitors.

- **Continual improvement:** ISO 9001 promotes a culture of continual improvement within organizations. By implementing the Plan-Do-Check-Act (PDCA) cycle, organizations continually monitor, measure, analyse, and evaluate their QMS. This iterative process allows organizations to identify areas for improvement, implement corrective actions, and proactively address potential issues. Continual improvement leads to increased efficiency, better product quality, enhanced customer satisfaction, and the ability to adapt to changing market conditions.

Obtaining ISO 9001 certification is a significant achievement that signals an organization's dedication to quality management and excellence. It demonstrates a commitment to meeting customer expectations, continuous improvement, and adherence to globally recognized standards. ISO 9001 certification can enhance an organization's reputation, credibility, and market competitiveness, leading to increased customer satisfaction, improved operational performance, and sustained business success.

Chapter 8: ISO 23635: Distributed Ledger Technology Governance

8.1 Exploring ISO 23635 Standard

ISO 23635 provides guidance for the governance of distributed ledger technology (DLT), including blockchain. As DLT gains prominence across various industries, the standard helps organizations establish effective governance practices to ensure the integrity, security, and interoperability of DLT systems.

8.1.1 The Need for DLT Governance

DLT governance is crucial to address the unique challenges and risks associated with the technology. As DLT involves decentralized networks, multiple participants, and immutable records, effective governance ensures that the technology operates in a trusted and secure manner.

8.1.2 Key Principles of DLT Governance

The ISO 23635 standard is built upon a set of key principles that guide organizations in governing DLT effectively. These principles include:

- **Accountability:** DLT governance requires establishing clear roles, responsibilities, and decision-making processes to ensure accountability among stakeholders. This involves defining the roles of network participants, such as validators, miners, and node operators, and establishing mechanisms for decision-making, conflict resolution, and dispute settlement. By ensuring accountability, organizations can foster trust and confidence in the DLT system and its participants.

- **Integrity:** Maintaining the integrity of data, transactions, and DLT systems is crucial for effective governance. Measures should be in place to prevent unauthorized modifications, tampering, or manipulation of data within the DLT system. This includes implementing cryptographic algorithms, consensus mechanisms, and mechanisms to detect and mitigate attacks or malicious activities. Ensuring data integrity helps maintain the trustworthiness of the DLT system and the information stored within it.

- **Security:** Robust security controls and mechanisms should be implemented to protect DLT systems from unauthorized access, fraud, and cyber threats. This includes measures such as secure key management, encryption, access controls, and secure coding practices. Additionally, organizations should establish incident response plans, conduct regular security assessments, and stay updated on emerging threats and vulnerabilities. Strong security practices help safeguard the DLT system and the assets and data it holds.

- **Transparency:** DLT governance should promote transparency by providing visibility into the rules, processes, and changes within the network. This includes making the governance framework, consensus mechanisms, and smart contracts accessible and understandable to participants. Transparent governance fosters trust, enables participants to make informed decisions, and promotes accountability. It also allows stakeholders to verify the compliance of the DLT system with relevant standards and regulations.

- **Interoperability:** DLT systems should be designed to enable interoperability and seamless integration with other systems and networks. Interoperability allows different DLT platforms or networks to communicate, share data, and transact with each other. This is particularly important as DLT adoption grows, and organizations need to collaborate across different platforms. Interoperable DLT systems enhance efficiency, reduce friction, and expand the potential use cases and benefits of DLT technology.

By adhering to these principles, organizations can establish governance frameworks that address the unique characteristics and requirements of DLT. Effective DLT governance ensures that DLT systems operate in a trusted, secure, and interoperable manner, promoting the integrity of data and transactions. It also fosters accountability, transparency, and confidence among participants, enabling the realization of the full potential of DLT technology.

8.2 Governance Considerations for Blockchain and DLT:

8.2.1 Decision-Making Structures:

Effective governance of blockchain and DLT involves establishing decision-making structures that ensure consensus among participants. These structures may vary depending on the DLT network and its governance model. Common decision-making structures include:

- **Governing Body:** A governing body, such as a board of directors or a consortium, may be responsible for making strategic decisions related to the governance of the DLT network. This body sets the direction, establishes policies, and makes high-level decisions that impact the network's operations.

- **Working Groups or Technical Committees:** Working groups or technical committees comprised of relevant stakeholders, such as developers, users, and subject matter experts, can be established to make decisions on specific technical or operational aspects of the DLT network. These groups contribute to the development and evolution of the DLT system, ensuring that diverse perspectives and expertise are considered.

The decision-making structures aim to facilitate collaboration, consensus-building, and effective governance by ensuring that decisions are made collectively and reflect the interests and expertise of the stakeholders involved.

8.2.2 Technical Standards and Protocols:

Governance of DLT often involves the establishment of technical standards and protocols that define the rules, formats, and interfaces for DLT operations. These standards serve several purposes:

- **Interoperability:** Technical standards ensure that different DLT networks or platforms can communicate and interact with each other seamlessly. They define common protocols and interfaces, enabling interoperability and facilitating the exchange of data and assets across different networks.

- **Security and Consistency:** Standards establish guidelines for implementing security measures, cryptographic algorithms, and protocols that protect the integrity and confidentiality of transactions and data within the DLT network. They also ensure consistency in data formats, ensuring that information is uniformly represented and interpreted across the network.

- **Scalability and Performance:** Standards can address scalability and performance challenges, providing guidelines for optimizing the efficiency and speed of DLT networks. They define best practices for network architecture, consensus mechanisms, and transaction processing to enhance the overall performance of the system.

Developing and adhering to technical standards and protocols is essential for promoting interoperability, enhancing security, and ensuring the reliability and trustworthiness of DLT networks.

8.2.3 Legal and Regulatory Compliance:

DLT governance should address legal and regulatory requirements to ensure compliance. Organizations need to consider applicable laws, data privacy regulations, anti-money laundering measures, and other legal considerations when designing their DLT governance frameworks. Key considerations include:

Data Privacy: DLT networks may involve the storage and sharing of sensitive personal data. Organizations need to comply with relevant data protection regulations, such as the General Data Protection Regulation (GDPR), by implementing appropriate data protection measures and ensuring individuals' rights are respected.

- **Anti-Money Laundering (AML) and Know Your Customer (KYC):** Organizations involved in DLT networks that deal with financial transactions or digital assets must comply with AML and KYC regulations. They need to establish proper identity verification processes, transaction monitoring, and reporting mechanisms to prevent money laundering and terrorist financing activities.

- **Intellectual Property Rights:** Organizations should consider intellectual property rights associated with the use of DLT. They need to ensure that intellectual property is protected and that any intellectual property licensing or usage agreements are properly documented and enforced.

By addressing legal and regulatory compliance, organizations can minimize legal risks, build trust among participants, and ensure the sustainable operation of DLT networks.

8.2.4 Risk Management:

Effective governance of DLT requires robust risk management practices. Organizations should identify and assess risks associated with DLT, including cybersecurity risks, data breaches, and operational vulnerabilities. Key aspects of DLT risk management include:

- **Risk Identification:** Organizations should identify and evaluate risks associated with the use of DLT technology. This includes assessing cybersecurity threats, vulnerabilities in the DLT network, and operational risks related to performance, scalability, and data integrity.

- **Risk Mitigation:** Mitigation strategies and controls should be implemented to address identified risks. This may involve implementing strong cybersecurity measures, conducting regular security audits, establishing backup and recovery mechanisms, and implementing disaster recovery plans.

- **Incident Response:** Organizations should establish incident response plans to address potential incidents or breaches within the DLT network. This includes procedures for detecting, reporting, and responding to security incidents, as well as mechanisms for communication, investigation, and resolution.

By adopting a proactive approach to risk management, organizations can effectively mitigate risks, protect the integrity of the DLT network, and ensure the continuity of operations.

By considering these governance aspects, organizations can establish effective frameworks that promote consensus, interoperability, security, legal compliance, and risk management in their DLT networks. These considerations ensure the smooth and trustworthy operation of DLT systems, fostering confidence and facilitating the adoption of DLT technology in various industries.8.3 Addressing Risk and Compliance in DLT Environments

DLT governance should include mechanisms for addressing risk and compliance. Organizations need to establish processes for monitoring and assessing risks associated with DLT, implementing controls to mitigate risks, and ensuring compliance with relevant laws and regulations.

This includes establishing procedures for data protection, cybersecurity, identity verification, and auditability of transactions. Regular risk assessments and compliance audits help organizations identify vulnerabilities, address gaps, and continuously improve their DLT governance practices.

8.4 Leveraging ISO 23635 for Effective Governance in Blockchain Projects

ISO 23635 provides a valuable framework for organizations

undertaking blockchain projects. By adopting the standard, organizations can ensure the governance of their blockchain networks is aligned with industry best practices and recognized principles.

ISO 23635 helps organizations address the unique challenges of blockchain governance, such as consensus mechanisms, decentralized decision-making, and interoperability. It provides guidance on establishing governance structures, defining roles and responsibilities, ensuring data integrity, and managing risks associated with blockchain technology.

By leveraging ISO 23635, organizations can enhance the trust, transparency, and effectiveness of their blockchain projects, ultimately driving adoption and unlocking the full potential of this transformative technology.

Chapter 9: ISO 37301: Compliance Management Systems

9.1 Overview of ISO 37301 Standard

ISO 37301 provides guidance for establishing, implementing, maintaining, and improving compliance management systems within organizations. The standard assists organizations in developing a systematic and proactive approach to compliance, ensuring adherence to laws, regulations, and internal policies.

9.2 Developing an Effective Compliance Management System

To establish an effective compliance management system,

organizations should consider the following key elements:

- **Leadership commitment:** Top management plays a crucial role in establishing and maintaining an effective compliance management system. They should demonstrate commitment by establishing a compliance policy that sets the organization's expectations and commitment to compliance. Top management should allocate resources, including personnel and financial resources, to support compliance efforts. By fostering a culture of compliance, top management encourages employees at all levels to prioritize compliance and make it an integral part of their daily activities.

- **Compliance objectives and planning:** Organizations need to define compliance objectives that align with their overall goals and values. This involves identifying and understanding applicable legal and regulatory requirements that the organization must comply with. Organizations should conduct a compliance gap analysis to determine any areas of non-compliance and develop a compliance plan to address those gaps. The compliance plan should outline the actions, resources, and timelines required to achieve and maintain compliance.

- **Compliance controls and measures:** To mitigate compliance risks, organizations should implement controls and measures. This includes establishing policies, procedures, and guidelines that outline expected behaviours and actions to ensure compliance. Controls may involve segregation of duties, approval processes, and access controls to prevent unauthorized activities. Organizations should also implement monitoring mechanisms, such as audits and regular assessments, to verify compliance with applicable requirements. The implementation of compliance controls and measures helps to prevent and detect non-compliance issues and maintain a proactive approach to compliance.

- **Compliance monitoring and review:** Regular monitoring and review activities are essential to assess the effectiveness of compliance controls and measures. This involves conducting internal audits, assessments, or evaluations to evaluate compliance performance. Monitoring and review activities help identify areas for improvement, address non-compliance issues, and ensure that the compliance management system remains up to date and effective. It also provides an opportunity to make necessary adjustments to compliance controls and measures in response to changes in laws, regulations, or the organizational environment.

- **Compliance communication and training:** Effective communication and training programs are vital for promoting awareness of compliance requirements and fostering a culture of compliance. Organizations should establish communication channels to provide guidance on compliance-related matters, such as distributing compliance policies and procedures, issuing regular compliance updates, and facilitating the reporting of compliance concerns. Training programs should be implemented to educate employees on their compliance responsibilities, provide them with the necessary skills and knowledge to comply with requirements, and emphasize the importance of ethical behaviour and integrity.

- **Compliance documentation and records:** Comprehensive documentation and records are essential components of a compliance management system. Organizations should maintain written policies, procedures, and guidelines that document their compliance requirements and expectations.

Additionally, organizations should keep records of compliance-related activities, such as training records, audit reports, incident reports, and evidence of compliance. Documentation and records serve as evidence of the organization's commitment to compliance, facilitate audits and assessments, and enable effective communication and reporting on compliance matters.

By considering these key elements and incorporating them into their compliance management systems, organizations can establish a robust framework for managing compliance risks, ensuring adherence to legal and regulatory requirements, and fostering a culture of compliance throughout the organization.

9.3 Aligning Compliance with Organizational Objectives and Governance Practices

Compliance management systems should be aligned with an organization's overall objectives and governance practices. By integrating compliance into the organization's governance framework, organizations ensure that compliance requirements are considered in decision-making processes and that compliance risks are effectively managed.

Alignment with governance practices enables organizations to establish clear roles and responsibilities, promote accountability, and foster a culture of compliance throughout the organization. It also facilitates the integration of compliance controls into operational processes, ensuring that compliance becomes an integral part of everyday activities.

9.4 Continuous Improvement and Auditing for Compliance

ISO 37301 emphasizes the importance of continuous improvement in compliance management. Organizations should regularly assess the effectiveness of their compliance management systems, identify areas for improvement, and take corrective actions to enhance their compliance capabilities.

Internal and external audits play a crucial role in verifying the effectiveness of compliance management systems. By conducting periodic audits, organizations can evaluate their compliance performance, identify non-compliance issues, and implement corrective measures to address any gaps or weaknesses.

Compliance audits provide organizations with independent assurance that their compliance management systems are functioning effectively and in accordance with applicable requirements. They also serve as a mechanism for demonstrating due diligence to regulators, stakeholders, and interested parties.

By implementing ISO 37301 and adopting a proactive approach to compliance management, organizations can enhance their ability to meet legal and regulatory requirements, reduce compliance risks, and build trust and confidence among stakeholders.

Chapter 10: ISO/IEC 38505: Governance of IT Enabled Investments

10.1 Introduction to ISO/IEC 38505 Standard

ISO/IEC 38505 provides guidance for the governance of IT-enabled investments, focusing on ensuring that organizations maximize the value derived from their IT investments. The standard emphasizes the need for effective decision-making, transparency, and accountability in managing IT-enabled investments.

10.2 Key Principles of Governance of IT-enabled Investments

The ISO/IEC 38505 standard is built upon a set of key principles that organizations should consider when governing IT-enabled investments:

- **Strategic alignment:** IT-enabled investments should be aligned with the organization's strategic objectives. This involves ensuring that investments support and contribute to the achievement of business goals. By aligning IT investments with strategic objectives, organizations can prioritize investments that have the most significant impact on the organization's overall performance and competitive advantage.

- **Value optimization:** Investments should be evaluated and prioritized based on their potential value and return on investment (ROI). Organizations should consider factors such as financial benefits, operational efficiency improvements, risk reduction, and strategic value when assessing the value of IT-enabled investments. By optimizing the value of investments, organizations can make more informed decisions about resource allocation and prioritize investments that offer the highest potential return.

- **Risk management:** Organizations need to assess and manage the risks associated with IT-enabled investments. This includes considering factors such as technology risks, project complexity, dependencies on external parties, and potential impacts on business operations. By conducting risk assessments, organizations can identify and mitigate potential risks, ensuring that investments are pursued with a clear understanding of associated risks and appropriate risk mitigation strategies in place.

- **Decision-making process:** Effective decision-making processes should be established to evaluate and select IT-enabled investments. This involves considering factors such as cost, benefits, alignment with strategic objectives, and risk assessments. Clear decision-making criteria and processes ensure that investment decisions are based on thorough analysis and evaluation, minimizing bias, and promoting transparency and accountability.

- **Stakeholder engagement:** Stakeholders should be involved and engaged throughout the investment lifecycle. This includes identifying and involving relevant stakeholders, such as business units, IT teams, executive leadership, and end-users, to provide their input, perspectives, and support during investment decision-making. Engaging stakeholders fosters buy-in, increases the likelihood of successful implementation, and ensures alignment between investment decisions and stakeholder expectations.

- **Performance monitoring:** Regular monitoring and evaluation of IT-enabled investments should be conducted to assess their performance, identify issues, and make necessary adjustments. This includes tracking key performance indicators (KPIs), measuring progress against established targets, and conducting periodic reviews of investment outcomes. By monitoring performance, organizations can identify areas for improvement, address any deviations from expected results, and make informed decisions regarding further investments or adjustments.

10.3 Governance Practices for IT-enabled Investments

Effective governance of IT-enabled investments involves implementing various practices throughout the investment lifecycle:

- **Investment identification and selection:** Organizations need to identify potential IT-enabled investments and assess their feasibility and alignment with strategic objectives. This involves conducting feasibility studies, cost-benefit analyses, and risk assessments to evaluate investment options. Selecting investments with the highest value and potential return helps organizations prioritize their resources and focus on initiatives that align with their strategic goals.

- **Investment planning and execution:** Detailed plans, budgets, and project management practices should be established to ensure the effective execution of IT-enabled investments. This includes defining project scope, timelines, resource allocation, and risk mitigation strategies. Effective planning and execution practices help organizations stay on track, manage resources efficiently, and mitigate risks throughout the investment lifecycle.

- **Performance monitoring and evaluation:** Regular monitoring and evaluation of IT-enabled investments should be conducted to assess their performance against established targets. This involves tracking KPIs, evaluating project milestones, and conducting periodic reviews. Performance monitoring and evaluation provide insights into the progress, success, or potential challenges of investments, enabling organizations to make informed decisions and take corrective actions as needed.

- **Benefit realization and optimization:** Organizations should actively manage and optimize the benefits derived from IT-enabled investments. This involves aligning investment outcomes with expected benefits, tracking, and measuring benefits realization, and taking actions to maximize their impact. Benefit realization and optimization ensure that investments deliver the intended value and contribute to the organization's overall objectives.

- **Governance and decision-making structures:** Clear governance structures and decision-making processes should be established for IT-enabled investment governance. This includes defining roles, responsibilities, and accountability for decision-making, establishing governance committees or boards, and ensuring appropriate communication and reporting channels. Clear governance structures promote transparency, enable effective decision-making, and ensure alignment with organizational objectives.

- **Continuous improvement:** Lessons learned from previous IT-enabled investments should be captured and applied to improve future investment decisions and governance practices.

This involves conducting post-implementation reviews, capturing feedback and insights, and updating governance processes based on lessons learned. Continuous improvement ensures that organizations evolve their governance practices, optimize decision-making, and enhance the success of future investments.

By implementing these governance principles and practices, organizations can enhance their ability to make informed investment decisions, optimize the value derived from IT-enabled investments, and align their IT investments with strategic objectives. These practices promote effective governance, risk management, and performance monitoring throughout the investment lifecycle, enabling organizations to maximize the benefits and value of their IT investments.

Chapter 11: ISO 55001: Asset Management

11.1 Overview of ISO 55001 Standard

ISO 55001 provides a framework for implementing an effective asset management system within an organization. The standard focuses on the management of physical assets, such as equipment, facilities, and infrastructure, throughout their lifecycle to achieve value for the organization and its stakeholders.

11.2 Key Principles of Asset Management

ISO 55001 is based on a set of key principles that guide organizations in effectively managing their assets:

- **Value creation:** The primary objective of asset management is to create value for the organization and its stakeholders. This involves considering both financial and non-financial aspects of assets. Organizations should strive to optimize the value generated by their assets through effective asset management practices, such as maximizing asset performance, minimizing costs, and enhancing asset utilization.

- **Alignment with organizational objectives:** Asset management should be aligned with the organization's overall objectives. This ensures that asset management strategies, activities, and decisions are directed towards supporting the achievement of strategic goals. Assets should be managed in a way that contributes to the organization's mission, vision, and long-term sustainability.

- **Leadership and commitment:** Top management plays a crucial role in asset management by demonstrating leadership and commitment. They should establish a culture of asset management throughout the organization, promote asset management policies and objectives, allocate resources for asset management activities, and provide guidance and support to employees involved in asset management efforts.

- **Lifecycle perspective:** Assets should be managed throughout their lifecycle, from acquisition to disposal. This includes considering activities such as design, operation, maintenance, and renewal. Effective asset management requires a holistic approach that encompasses the entire lifecycle of assets, ensuring their optimal performance, reliability, and cost-effectiveness over time.

- **Risk management:** Organizations need to identify and manage risks associated with asset management. This includes risks related to safety, performance, compliance, and environmental impacts. Risk management practices should be integrated into asset management processes, ensuring that risks are identified, assessed, and mitigated to prevent or minimize potential adverse impacts on asset performance, safety, and organizational objectives.

- **Performance evaluation and improvement:** Regular performance evaluation should be conducted to assess asset performance, identify areas for improvement, and implement measures to enhance asset management effectiveness. This involves establishing performance indicators, measuring, and analysing asset performance data, and using the insights gained to drive continuous improvement in asset management practices and outcomes.

11.3 Implementing an Asset Management System

To implement an effective asset management system, organizations should consider the following key components:

- **Context of the organization:** Organizations need to understand the internal and external factors that influence asset management. This includes considering stakeholder needs and expectations, regulatory requirements, industry standards, and operational considerations. Understanding the context helps organizations develop asset management strategies and plans that are aligned with the organization's specific circumstances and goals.

- **Leadership and commitment:** Top management should provide leadership and demonstrate commitment to asset management. This involves establishing asset management policies that define the organization's approach and objectives, allocating resources for asset management activities, and actively participating in decision-making processes related to asset management.

- **Planning:** Organizations need to develop asset management plans that outline objectives, strategies, and activities to achieve desired asset performance and value. Asset management plans should cover areas such as asset acquisition, operation, maintenance, and disposal. The plans should be aligned with the organization's overall goals and consider the organization's context, risk appetite, and available resources.

- **Support:** Adequate resources, including personnel, information systems, and infrastructure, should be provided to support the asset management system. This includes ensuring that competent personnel are available to carry out asset management activities, appropriate information systems are in place to capture and analyse asset data, and necessary infrastructure is available to support asset operations and maintenance.

- **Operation:** Asset management processes should be established and executed to ensure effective asset management. This includes activities such as asset acquisition, operation, maintenance, and disposal. Processes should be documented, standardized, and communicated to relevant personnel to ensure consistent and reliable asset management practices across the organization.

- **Performance evaluation:** Organizations should monitor and measure asset performance, assess compliance with requirements, and evaluate the effectiveness of the asset management system. This involves establishing performance indicators and metrics, collecting and analysing data on asset performance, and conducting periodic evaluations and audits to assess the organization's adherence to asset management objectives and standards.

- **Improvement:** Based on performance evaluation results, organizations should identify areas for improvement, establish corrective actions, and implement changes to enhance asset management effectiveness. Continual improvement is a fundamental principle of asset management. Lessons learned from performance evaluations, feedback from stakeholders, and changing business needs should be used to drive ongoing improvement in asset management practices and outcomes.

By considering these key principles and implementing the key components of an asset management system, organizations can enhance their ability to create value from their assets, align asset management with organizational objectives, effectively manage risks, and continually improve their asset management practices.

11.4 Benefits of ISO 55001 Certification for Organizations

ISO 55001 certification offers several benefits to organizations, including:

- **Improved asset performance and reliability:** Effective asset management, as guided by ISO 55001, helps organizations optimize the performance and reliability of their assets. By implementing best practices in asset management, organizations can enhance asset maintenance practices, improve asset uptime, and reduce the frequency and impact of asset failures. This leads to increased operational efficiency, improved productivity, and a reduction in costly downtime.

- **Enhanced decision-making:** ISO 55001 provides organizations with a systematic approach to collecting and analysing asset data. By implementing the standard's requirements, organizations can establish processes for capturing accurate and reliable asset information, such as asset condition, performance, and lifecycle data. This data-driven approach enables informed decision-making regarding asset acquisition, maintenance strategies, and renewal activities. Organizations can prioritize investments, allocate resources effectively, and make informed choices based on a comprehensive understanding of asset performance and condition.

- **Cost savings and risk reduction:** Effective asset management, as facilitated by ISO 55001, enables organizations to achieve cost savings and risk reduction. By managing assets effectively, organizations can reduce costs associated with asset failures, unplanned maintenance, and unnecessary asset purchases. Through proactive asset maintenance and risk mitigation strategies, organizations can minimize the likelihood and impact of asset-related incidents, safety hazards, and non-compliance. This helps reduce financial losses, regulatory penalties, and reputational risks.

- **Alignment with best practices:** ISO 55001 certification demonstrates an organization's adherence to international best practices in asset management. By aligning their asset management practices with the requirements of the standard, organizations can demonstrate their commitment to implementing proven methodologies, processes, and systems for managing assets. This enhances credibility and trust among stakeholders, including customers, investors, regulators, and business partners. ISO 55001 certification serves as evidence that the organization follows recognized industry standards for effective asset management.

- **Continuous improvement:** Implementing ISO 55001 promotes a culture of continuous improvement in asset management practices. The standard emphasizes the importance of regular performance evaluations, analysis of data, and the identification of areas for improvement. Through periodic reviews and audits, organizations can identify opportunities for enhancing asset management practices, optimizing maintenance strategies, and implementing corrective actions. This culture of continuous improvement ensures that asset management practices evolve over time, resulting in increased efficiency, effectiveness, and adaptability to changing business needs.

ISO 55001 certification serves as a testament to an organization's commitment to effective asset management. It demonstrates that the organization has implemented a robust asset management system aligned with international best practices. The benefits of certification include improved asset performance, enhanced decision-making, cost savings, risk reduction, alignment with industry standards, and a culture of continuous improvement. ISO 55001 certification contributes to improved organizational performance, stakeholder satisfaction, and long-term sustainability by ensuring assets are managed in a way that maximizes their value and supports the organization's objectives.

Chapter 12: ISO 27001: Information Security and Governance

12.1 Introduction to ISO 27001

Information security is a critical aspect of organizational governance. ISO 27001 is an international standard that provides a framework for establishing, implementing, maintaining, and continually improving an information security management system (ISMS). This chapter explores the importance of ISO 27001 in the context of governance and highlights key considerations for implementing effective information security practices.

12.2 The Role of Governance in Information Security

Governance plays a vital role in ensuring the confidentiality, integrity, and availability of information within an organization. It provides the necessary structure, policies, and processes to manage information security risks and protect valuable assets. ISO 27001 aligns with governance principles by emphasizing the need for clear roles, responsibilities, and accountability for information security at all levels of the organization.

12.3 Understanding ISO 27001 Information Security Standard

ISO 27001 provides a comprehensive framework for establishing an ISMS that addresses the organization's information security risks. The standard encompasses various areas, including risk assessment and treatment, security controls implementation, incident management, and continual improvement. It enables organizations to adopt a systematic and risk-based approach to managing information security.

12.4 Benefits of adopting the Information Security Standard

Implementing ISO 27001 brings several benefits to an organization. These include:

- **Enhanced Information Security:** Implementing ISO 27001 helps organizations identify and mitigate information security risks. The standard provides a systematic approach to assessing security risks, implementing controls, and managing the confidentiality, integrity, and availability of sensitive information. By following the standard's requirements, organizations can establish robust information security practices, safeguarding sensitive data from unauthorized access, disclosure, alteration, or destruction. This contributes to the overall protection of valuable information assets and reduces the likelihood of security breaches and data loss.

- **Compliance with Legal and Regulatory Requirements:** ISO 27001 assists organizations in meeting legal, regulatory, and contractual requirements related to information security. The standard provides a framework that enables organizations to identify applicable laws, regulations, and industry-specific requirements pertaining to information security. By implementing ISO 27001, organizations can align their information security practices with these requirements, demonstrating a systematic and proactive approach to fulfilling their obligations. This helps organizations avoid legal and regulatory penalties, contractual non-compliance, and reputational damage associated with information security breaches.

- **Increased Stakeholder Trust:** By demonstrating a commitment to information security through ISO 27001 certification, organizations can enhance stakeholder confidence and build trust with customers, partners, and suppliers. ISO 27001 certification serves as evidence that the organization has implemented internationally recognized best practices for information security. It provides assurance to stakeholders that their sensitive information is being handled securely and that the organization is actively managing information security risks. This increased trust can lead to stronger relationships with stakeholders, improved customer satisfaction, and enhanced business opportunities.

- **Competitive Advantage:** ISO 27001 certification can provide a competitive edge by differentiating the organization as a trusted and secure partner. In today's digital landscape, information security is a critical concern for organizations and their stakeholders. By obtaining ISO 27001 certification, organizations can demonstrate their commitment to protecting sensitive information, which can be a compelling factor for customers, partners, and suppliers when selecting a business partner. ISO 27001 certification can give organizations a competitive advantage by instilling confidence in their security practices, positioning them as a reliable and trustworthy organization in the marketplace.

- **Continual Improvement:** ISO 27001 promotes a culture of continual improvement in information security. The standard emphasizes the importance of regular review, assessment, and updating of information security controls and practices. By implementing ISO 27001, organizations establish processes for monitoring and evaluating the effectiveness of their information security measures, identifying areas for improvement, and implementing necessary changes. This iterative approach ensures that information security practices remain relevant, robust, and aligned with emerging threats, technology advancements, and changing business needs.

By adopting the ISO 27001 Information Security Standard, organizations can enhance their information security posture, meet regulatory requirements, build stakeholder trust, gain a competitive advantage, and foster a culture of continual improvement in information security practices.

12.5 Integrating ISO 27001 with Governance Practices

Effective governance involves the establishment of structures, processes, and practices that guide decision-making, ensure accountability, and align activities with strategic objectives. Information security is a critical aspect of governance, as it involves protecting sensitive information, managing risks, and ensuring the continuity of business operations.

ISO 27001 provides a framework for establishing and maintaining an information security management system (ISMS). This system enables organizations to identify, assess, and manage information security risks systematically. By integrating ISO 27001 with governance practices, organizations can align their information security objectives with overall business objectives and ensure that information security receives appropriate attention at the governance level.

Achieving ISO 27001 integration with core governance

practices:

- **Governance Structure:** The organization's governance structure should include information security as a key component. This can be achieved by establishing an Information Security Steering Committee or including information security responsibilities within existing governance bodies. These structures should have representation from top management, information security professionals, and key stakeholders to ensure appropriate oversight and decision-making.

- **Policies and Procedures:** Governance frameworks typically include the development and implementation of policies and procedures that guide organizational activities. When integrating ISO 27001, organizations should develop and align information security policies and procedures with the overall governance framework. This ensures that information security objectives, responsibilities, and controls are clearly defined and communicated throughout the organization.

- **Risk Management:** Risk management is an integral part of both governance and ISO 27001. Integrating these practices involves aligning the risk management processes to account for information security risks. This includes identifying and assessing information security risks, integrating risk treatment plans into overall risk management practices, and regularly reviewing and updating risk assessments to reflect changes in the information security landscape.

- **Compliance and Audit:** Governance frameworks often include compliance requirements and internal auditing processes. Integrating ISO 27001 with governance practices involves incorporating information security compliance requirements, such as legal and regulatory obligations, into the governance framework. Internal audits should assess the effectiveness of the ISMS and ensure compliance with ISO 27001 requirements, contributing to overall governance assurance.

- **Performance Monitoring and Reporting:** Governance frameworks require performance monitoring and reporting mechanisms. Integrating ISO 27001 involves establishing information security performance indicators and including them in the overall performance monitoring and reporting processes. This ensures that information security is considered in the organization's performance evaluation and enables the identification of areas for improvement.

By integrating ISO 27001 with governance practices, organizations can establish a holistic approach to information security management. This integration ensures that information security considerations are embedded in decision-making processes, risk management activities, policy development, compliance requirements, and performance monitoring. It strengthens the organization's ability to protect critical assets, meet regulatory obligations, and align information security objectives with strategic goals, contributing to effective governance and the overall success of the organization.

Chapter 13: ISO 37000: Organization Change Management

13.1 Understanding ISO 37000 Standard

ISO 37000 is a standard that provides guidance on organization change management (OCM). It aims to help organizations effectively manage change initiatives to achieve desired outcomes while minimizing negative impacts on individuals and the organization.

13.2 Importance of Change Management in Governance

Change is an inherent part of organizational growth and adaptation. Effective change management is crucial for the success of governance initiatives:

- **Alignment with strategy:** Change management ensures that governance changes are aligned with the organization's strategic objectives. It helps stakeholders understand the rationale behind the changes, reducing resistance and increasing support for governance initiatives.

- **Minimizing disruption:** Change can create uncertainty and disruption within an organization. Effective change management helps mitigate these impacts by providing a structured approach to managing and communicating changes, reducing productivity losses and employee resistance.

- **Maximizing benefits realization:** Change management ensures that governance changes are implemented in a way that maximizes the realization of intended benefits. It helps organizations identify potential barriers and risks, develop mitigation strategies, and track progress toward desired outcomes.

13.3 Key Components and Practices for Effective Change Management

ISO 37000 outlines key components and practices for effective change management:

- **Change management governance:** Organizations should establish a change management governance structure that defines roles, responsibilities, and decision-making processes. This includes appointing change management sponsors, champions, and a change management team responsible for overseeing and implementing change initiatives. The governance structure ensures clear accountability, ownership, and support for change efforts throughout the organization. It facilitates effective coordination, communication, and decision-making to drive successful change implementation.

- **Change impact assessment:** Organizations should conduct a comprehensive assessment of the impacts of proposed changes on people, processes, systems, and the organization. This assessment helps identify potential risks, barriers, and required resources for successful change implementation. It involves analysing the scope of the change, assessing the potential consequences, and understanding how the change will affect different stakeholders. The impact assessment informs the development of appropriate change strategies, resource allocation, and risk mitigation plans.

- **Change communication and engagement:** Effective communication is critical for change success. Organizations should develop a communication plan that ensures consistent, timely, and targeted communication to all stakeholders. The plan should consider the appropriate channels, messages, and frequency of communication. Engaging stakeholders throughout the change process is equally important. This involves involving them in the change planning, seeking their input and feedback, addressing their concerns, and creating a sense of ownership and commitment to the change. Clear and transparent communication fosters trust, reduces resistance, and promotes a positive change culture.

- **Change readiness and capability building:** Organizations should assess their readiness and capacity for change. This includes evaluating the organization's change management capabilities, identifying skill gaps, and providing training and support to build the necessary competencies within the organization. Readiness assessment involves evaluating the organization's culture, leadership support, change infrastructure, and employee readiness for change. Capability building involves providing training on change management methodologies, tools, and techniques, and empowering employees to become change agents. Building change readiness and capabilities enhances the organization's capacity to effectively plan, execute, and sustain change initiatives.

- **Change implementation and monitoring:** Change initiatives should be implemented using a phased approach, with clear milestones and performance indicators. This allows for a structured and manageable transition. The implementation plan should outline specific activities, timelines, and resource requirements. Regular monitoring and feedback mechanisms should be established to track progress, identify deviations, and make necessary adjustments to ensure successful change adoption. Monitoring involves evaluating the effectiveness of change interventions, identifying barriers or resistance, and taking corrective actions when required. Continuous monitoring and feedback support timely decision-making and help ensure that change initiatives stay on track.

- **Change evaluation and learning:** After the implementation of changes, organizations should evaluate the effectiveness of the change management process. This evaluation assesses whether the desired outcomes have been achieved, the effectiveness of change strategies and interventions, and the overall success of the change effort. Lessons learned should be captured, documented, and used to improve future change initiatives. Continuous learning and improvement are essential for building change management capabilities within the organization. Organizations should foster a culture of reflection, adaptability, and continuous improvement, leveraging insights from previous changes to enhance future change initiatives.

By implementing the components and practices outlined in ISO 37000, organizations can establish a structured and effective change management approach. This ensures that change initiatives are aligned with strategic objectives, effectively communicated, and supported by stakeholders. It minimizes disruption, maximizes benefits realization, and builds change readiness and capabilities within the organization. Effective change management enhances organizational agility, adaptability, and long-term success in a dynamic business environment.

13.4 Integrating Change Management into Governance Frameworks

Change management and governance are interconnected processes that should work in harmony to drive successful organizational change and ensure effective governance practices. Integrating change management into governance frameworks helps organizations navigate and manage change effectively while ensuring alignment with overall governance objectives. Here are the key considerations for integrating change management into governance frameworks:

- **Change impact assessment:** When implementing governance initiatives, organizations should conduct a change impact assessment to understand the impacts on the organization's structure, processes, systems, and people. This assessment helps identify the changes required in governance practices to support the overall organizational change efforts. By considering the specific impacts on governance, organizations can ensure that governance frameworks and practices are updated and aligned with the changing organizational landscape.

- **Stakeholder engagement:** Effective governance requires engaging stakeholders at all levels. Similarly, change management practices emphasize the importance of stakeholder involvement and buy-in. Integrating change management into governance frameworks means actively involving stakeholders in governance initiatives, seeking their input, addressing their concerns, and ensuring their support for the proposed governance changes. Stakeholder engagement fosters a sense of ownership, builds trust, and increases the likelihood of successful governance implementation.

- **Change communication:** Clear and timely communication is crucial for effective governance. Change management principles and practices can be applied to develop communication strategies that promote understanding, transparency, and alignment with governance objectives. Communication plans should be developed to ensure that stakeholders are kept informed about the governance changes, their rationale, and the expected impacts. Communication should be tailored to different stakeholder groups and utilize various channels to ensure effective dissemination of information.

- **Change evaluation:** Governance frameworks should include mechanisms to evaluate the effectiveness of governance changes and their impact on the organization. Integrating change management principles into governance evaluation processes allows organizations to assess the success of governance initiatives and identify areas for improvement. Evaluation methods such as surveys, interviews, or performance indicators can be used to collect feedback, measure the outcomes of governance changes, and assess their alignment with the intended objectives. This feedback loop enables organizations to continuously improve governance practices and ensure their effectiveness in supporting organizational goals.

By implementing ISO 37000 and integrating change management into governance frameworks, organizations can effectively manage the impact of governance changes on the organization and its stakeholders. This integration ensures that governance practices are aligned with organizational change efforts, stakeholder engagement is prioritized, communication is clear and transparent, and evaluation processes measure the effectiveness of governance initiatives. Ultimately, this integration enables organizations to successfully implement governance changes, maximize their benefits, and foster a culture of continuous improvement in governance practices.

Chapter 14: ISO 45001: Occupational Health and Safety Management

14.1 Introduction to ISO 45001 Standard

ISO 45001 is an internationally recognized standard that provides governance related guidelines for implementing an occupational health and safety management system (OHSMS). The standard aims to improve workplace safety, reduce workplace injuries and illnesses, and promote a safe and healthy working environment.

14.2 Key Elements of an OHSMS

ISO 45001 outlines several key elements that organizations should consider when implementing an OHSMS:

- **Hazard identification and risk assessment:** Organizations need to proactively identify workplace hazards and assess the associated risks. This involves conducting regular inspections, risk assessments, and involving employees in the identification and assessment process. By identifying hazards and assessing risks, organizations can implement appropriate controls to prevent incidents and promote a safe working environment.

- **Legal and regulatory compliance:** Organizations must comply with applicable health and safety laws, regulations, and standards. It is essential to establish processes for monitoring changes in legislation, assessing compliance, and implementing necessary controls to meet legal requirements. Compliance ensures that the organization operates within the boundaries of the law, reducing the risk of legal penalties and reputational damage.

- **Objectives and targets:** Organizations should set measurable health and safety objectives and targets aligned with the organization's overall goals. These objectives should address areas of improvement identified through hazard identification, risk assessment, and legal compliance. By setting clear objectives and targets, organizations can focus their efforts on improving specific health and safety aspects and track their progress over time.

- **Resources and competencies:** Adequate resources, including personnel, infrastructure, and training, should be provided to implement and maintain the OHSMS effectively. It is important to ensure that employees receive appropriate training and are competent to perform their assigned health and safety-related tasks. Competent employees are better equipped to identify hazards, follow safe work practices, and respond effectively in emergency situations.

- **Operational controls:** Organizations need to establish controls to mitigate health and safety risks. This includes implementing safe work procedures, providing personal protective equipment (PPE), conducting regular maintenance of equipment and machinery, and ensuring the availability of emergency response plans. Operational controls help prevent accidents, injuries, and illnesses by reducing exposure to hazards in the workplace.

- **Emergency preparedness and response:** Organizations should develop and implement emergency response plans, including procedures for evacuation, first aid, fire safety, and communication during emergencies. Regular drills and exercises should be conducted to test the effectiveness of emergency preparedness measures. Being prepared for emergencies minimizes the potential impact on employees, reduces response time, and helps prevent further harm.

- **Performance measurement and monitoring:** Organizations need to establish processes for measuring and monitoring health and safety performance. This includes collecting and analysing data on incidents, near-misses, and other relevant indicators. Performance indicators should be used to assess progress, identify trends, and drive continuous improvement. Monitoring performance allows organizations to identify areas of concern, evaluate the effectiveness of controls, and implement corrective actions to prevent incidents.

- **Worker participation and consultation:** Organizations should involve workers in health and safety decision-making processes. This includes consulting with workers, providing mechanisms for reporting health and safety concerns, and encouraging employee participation in hazard identification and risk assessment activities. Worker participation fosters a culture of shared responsibility and collaboration, as employees bring valuable insights and knowledge to the health and safety management process.

- **Management review:** Top management should conduct regular reviews of the OHSMS to evaluate its effectiveness, identify opportunities for improvement, and ensure its alignment with organizational goals and objectives. These reviews should consider performance data, employee feedback, and changes in legal and regulatory requirements. Management reviews provide a mechanism for continuous improvement and ensure that the OHSMS remains relevant and effective in addressing health and safety risks.

14.3 Benefits of ISO 45001 Certification for Organizations

Implementing ISO 45001 and achieving certification offers several benefits to organizations:

- **Enhanced workplace safety:** Implementing ISO 45001 focuses on identifying and mitigating workplace hazards, reducing the risk of accidents, injuries, and illnesses. This leads to a safer and healthier work environment for employees, promoting their well-being and productivity.

- **Compliance with legal requirements:** ISO 45001 helps organizations ensure compliance with applicable health and safety laws, regulations, and standards. Compliance reduces the risk of legal penalties, reputational damage, and business disruptions, reinforcing the organization's commitment to legal and regulatory obligations.

- **Improved employee morale and engagement:** A strong commitment to health and safety fosters a positive work culture, where employees feel valued and protected. This boosts employee morale and engagement, leading to increased productivity, job satisfaction, and retention.

- **Reduced costs:** By preventing workplace incidents and illnesses, organizations can avoid the associated costs of medical treatments, compensation claims, and disruptions to operations. Implementing effective health and safety controls can also lead to reduced insurance premiums, saving costs in the long run.

- **Competitive advantage:** ISO 45001 certification demonstrates an organization's commitment to workplace safety and health. It can enhance the organization's reputation, attract customers who prioritize safety, and differentiate the organization from competitors. ISO 45001 certification serves as a valuable credential, providing a competitive edge in the marketplace.

By implementing ISO 45001 and achieving certification, organizations can effectively manage occupational health and safety risks, protect their employees, and create a positive work environment. The benefits include safer workplaces, legal compliance, engaged employees, cost savings, and a competitive advantage.

14.4 Integration of OHSMS with Overall Governance Framework

Integrating the OHSMS with the organization's overall governance framework ensures that health and safety is given due consideration:

- **Leadership commitment:** Top management should demonstrate a strong commitment to health and safety by actively participating in the OHSMS and promoting a culture of safety throughout the organization. This includes setting clear health and safety objectives, providing necessary resources for implementation, and leading by example in adhering to health and safety practices. Leadership commitment helps establish a positive tone at the top and fosters employee engagement in health and safety initiatives.

- **Alignment with strategic objectives:** The OHSMS should align with the organization's strategic goals and objectives. Health and safety considerations should be integrated into the overall governance framework, ensuring that they are considered in decision-making processes, resource allocation, and operational planning. Aligning health and safety with strategic objectives ensures that it receives adequate attention and resources, and that health and safety goals are aligned with the organization's overall vision and mission.

- **Risk management:** Health and safety risks should be identified, assessed, and managed within the organization's risk management framework. This involves integrating health and safety risk assessments into the organization's overall risk management processes, considering health and safety risks in operational planning, project management, and resource allocation decisions. By incorporating health and safety risks into the broader risk management framework, organizations can prioritize and address health and safety concerns alongside other operational risks.

- **Performance measurement:** Health and safety performance indicators should be integrated into the organization's performance measurement system. This includes establishing metrics, targets, and reporting mechanisms to track health and safety performance and progress. Regular reporting and reviews should be conducted to assess the effectiveness of the OHSMS, identify areas for improvement, and communicate health and safety performance to stakeholders. Integrating health and safety performance measurement into the overall governance framework ensures that health and safety receives appropriate attention and evaluation at all levels of the organization.

- **Employee engagement:** Health and safety should be a shared responsibility, involving employees at all levels. Governance practices should encourage employee participation, consultation, and feedback on health and safety matters. This includes providing mechanisms for employees to report hazards, contribute to risk assessments, and participate in health and safety committees or forums. Engaging employees in health and safety decision-making promotes a culture of ownership, empowers employees to take responsibility for their own safety, and fosters a proactive approach to identifying and mitigating health and safety risks.

By integrating the OHSMS with the organization's overall governance framework, organizations can ensure that health and safety receives the necessary attention and resources to protect employees and create a safe working environment. Leadership commitment, alignment with strategic objectives, risk management integration, performance measurement, and employee engagement collectively strengthen the organization's approach to managing health and safety risks and promote a culture of safety throughout the organization.

Chapter 15: COBIT 2019: Governance and Management Framework

15.1 Overview of COBIT 2019

COBIT (Control Objectives for Information and Related Technologies) 2019 is a widely recognized framework for IT governance and management. It provides guidance to organizations on how to align their IT strategies with business objectives, optimize IT investments, and effectively manage IT-related risks. COBIT 2019 emphasizes the need for a comprehensive and integrated approach to IT governance, focusing on the key domains of Plan and Organize, Build, Acquire and Implement, Deliver and Support, and Monitor and Evaluate.

15.2 Key Principles and Framework Components

COBIT 2019 is based on a set of key principles that organizations should follow when implementing IT governance and management practices. These principles include:

- **Meeting Stakeholder Needs:** Organizations should understand and address the needs, expectations, and priorities of their stakeholders. This principle emphasizes the importance of actively engaging with stakeholders to define IT-related objectives and requirements and ensuring that IT activities are aligned with these needs.

- **Covering the Enterprise End-to-End:** COBIT 2019 promotes a holistic approach to IT governance and management. It recognizes that IT permeates all aspects of an organization and should be managed consistently across different functions and processes. This principle highlights the need to consider the end-to-end lifecycle of IT activities, from strategic planning to operational execution.

- **Applying a Single, Integrated Framework:** COBIT 2019 encourages organizations to adopt a single, integrated framework for IT governance and management. This principle promotes consistency and efficiency in managing IT processes and controls. By using a unified framework, organizations can avoid duplication of efforts and ensure that all relevant aspects of IT governance are addressed.

- **Enabling a Holistic Approach:** COBIT 2019 emphasizes the integration of various governance and management practices. It encourages organizations to align COBIT with other relevant frameworks and standards to create a comprehensive and integrated governance framework. This principle enables organizations to leverage synergies and ensure consistency in governance practices across different domains.

- **Separating Governance from Management:** COBIT 2019 distinguishes between governance and management activities. Governance focuses on decision-making, setting objectives, and providing oversight, while management focuses on execution and operational activities. This principle highlights the importance of clearly defining roles and responsibilities for effective IT governance.

Framework Components of COBIT 2019 include:

- **Governance and Management Objectives:** COBIT 2019 provides a set of objectives that organizations should strive to achieve in the context of IT governance and management. These objectives are categorized based on the five key domains of COBIT: Plan and Organize, Build, Acquire and Implement, Deliver and Support, and Monitor and Evaluate. Each objective is associated with specific performance indicators and aligns with business goals.

- **Governance and Management Practices:** COBIT 2019 defines a set of practices that organizations can implement to achieve the governance and management objectives. These practices provide detailed guidance on how to plan, implement, and monitor IT processes and controls. They cover a wide range of areas, including strategic alignment, risk management, resource optimization, performance measurement, and compliance.

- **Governance and Management Enablers:** COBIT 2019 identifies various enablers that support the implementation of governance and management practices. These enablers include policies, processes, organizational structures, culture, information, services, infrastructure, and people. They provide organizations with the necessary resources and capabilities to establish and sustain effective IT governance and management practices.

By adhering to the key principles and implementing the framework components outlined in COBIT 2019, organizations can establish a robust IT governance and management framework that aligns IT with business objectives, optimizes IT investments, manages IT-related risks, and ensures the delivery of value to stakeholders.

15.3 Integrating COBIT 2019 with Other Governance Standards and Practices

COBIT 2019 can be integrated with other governance standards and practices to create a comprehensive governance framework. For example, it can be aligned with ISO 38500 for corporate governance of IT, ISO 9001 for quality management, or ISO 27001 for information security management. Integration of COBIT 2019 with other standards allows organizations to leverage synergies and ensure consistency in governance practices across different domains. It enables a holistic approach to governance, where IT governance is aligned with overall organizational governance objectives.

Chapter 16: CMMI: Capability Maturity Model Integration

16.1 Overview of CMMI

CMMI (Capability Maturity Model Integration) is a framework that helps organizations enhance their capability and maturity in various domains, including process improvement and governance. It provides a set of best practices for managing and improving processes to achieve higher levels of performance, quality, and efficiency. CMMI focuses on establishing standardized processes, measuring performance, and continuously improving organizational capabilities.

16.2 Key Principles and Framework Components

CMMI is based on a set of key principles that organizations should follow when implementing process improvement and governance practices. These principles include:

- **Process Standardization:** CMMI emphasizes the need for standardizing processes across the organization. By defining and following standardized processes, organizations can reduce variations, improve efficiency, and ensure consistent and predictable outcomes.

- **Continuous Improvement:** CMMI promotes a culture of continuous improvement. It encourages organizations to regularly assess their processes, identify areas for enhancement, and implement changes to achieve better results. Continuous improvement drives organizational learning and agility, enabling organizations to adapt to changing business needs.

- **Measurement and Analysis:** CMMI highlights the importance of measuring process performance and analysing data to make informed decisions. By collecting and analysing relevant metrics, organizations can identify trends, monitor progress, and take proactive actions to address issues and drive improvement.

- **Organizational Learning:** CMMI recognizes the value of organizational learning and knowledge management. It emphasizes the need for capturing and sharing best practices, lessons learned, and organizational knowledge to foster innovation and improve performance.

Framework Components of CMMI include:

- **Process Areas:** CMMI defines a set of process areas that represent key areas of organizational focus. Each process area encompasses a set of practices that organizations should implement to achieve specific goals. Examples of process areas in CMMI include project management, requirements development, configuration management, and process improvement.

- **Maturity Levels:** CMMI defines five maturity levels that represent different stages of process capability and organizational maturity. These levels range from Initial (Level 1) to Optimizing (Level 5) and provide a roadmap for organizations to assess and improve their process performance. Each maturity level has specific criteria and requirements that organizations must fulfill to advance to the next level.

- **Capability Levels:** In addition to maturity levels, CMMI also defines capability levels that assess the capability of specific process areas. Capability levels range from Level 0 (Incomplete) to Level 5 (Optimizing). By evaluating the capability of different process areas, organizations can identify areas of strength and areas that require improvement.

By adhering to the key principles and implementing the framework components outlined in CMMI, organizations can enhance their process capability, improve performance, and drive continuous improvement.

16.3 Integrating CMMI with other Governance

Standards and Practices

CMMI can be integrated with other governance standards and practices to create a comprehensive governance framework. For example, it can be aligned with COBIT for IT governance and management, ISO 9001 for quality management, or ISO 27001 for information security management. Integration of CMMI with other standards allows organizations to leverage synergies and ensure consistency in governance practices across different domains. It enables a holistic approach to governance, where process improvement and governance practices are aligned with overall organizational governance objectives.

Chapter 17: OECD Principles of Corporate Governance

17.1 Overview of Principles of Corporate Governance

The OECD (Organization for Economic Cooperation and Development) Principles of Corporate Governance provide recommendations for good governance practices, with a focus on transparency, accountability, and equitable treatment of shareholders. These principles aim to enhance investor confidence, promote sustainable growth, and contribute to the stability of financial markets.

17.2 Key Principles and Framework Components

The OECD Principles of Corporate Governance consist of a set of key principles that organizations should adhere to when implementing corporate governance practices. These principles include:

- **Rights of Shareholders:** The OECD emphasizes the importance of protecting and facilitating the exercise of shareholders' rights. This principle promotes equitable treatment of shareholders, including minority and foreign shareholders. It highlights the need for transparent and timely disclosure of relevant information to shareholders, enabling them to make informed decisions and participate effectively in corporate governance processes.

- **Equitable Treatment of Shareholders:** The principle of equitable treatment emphasizes the fair treatment of all shareholders, regardless of their ownership stakes. It encourages organizations to establish mechanisms that prevent abusive actions, protect minority shareholders' rights, and ensure equal access to relevant information.

- **Role of Stakeholders:** The OECD recognizes the importance of considering the interests of stakeholders beyond shareholders. This principle promotes active engagement and dialogue with stakeholders, including employees, customers, suppliers, and the local community. It encourages organizations to establish mechanisms for stakeholder input, disclosure of relevant information, and responsible decision-making that considers the interests of various stakeholders.

- **Disclosure and Transparency:** The OECD emphasizes the need for transparent and accurate disclosure of financial and non-financial information. This principle promotes timely and comprehensive reporting to shareholders and other stakeholders. It highlights the importance of disclosure in building trust, facilitating market discipline, and enabling effective monitoring of corporate performance and governance.

- **Responsibilities of the Board:** The principle of board responsibilities focuses on the role of the board of directors in ensuring effective corporate governance. It emphasizes the need for competent and independent directors who act in the best interests of the company and its shareholders. The board should provide strategic guidance, oversee management, and establish effective internal controls and risk management systems.

- **The Role of Institutional Investors:** The OECD recognizes the influential role of institutional investors in corporate governance. This principle encourages institutional investors to actively engage with companies, exercise their voting rights, and promote good governance practices. It highlights the importance of long-term investment perspectives and responsible investment behaviour.

Framework Components of OECD Principles of Corporate Governance include:

- **Governance Structures and Processes:** The framework emphasizes the establishment of effective governance structures and processes that align with the OECD principles. This includes the composition and independence of the board of directors, the establishment of board committees, and the implementation of sound internal control and risk management systems.

- **Reporting and Disclosure Requirements:** The framework outlines reporting and disclosure requirements that organizations should follow to ensure transparency and accountability. This includes financial reporting, non-financial reporting (e.g., sustainability reporting), and the disclosure of governance-related information.

- **Stakeholder Engagement Mechanisms:** The framework encourages organizations to establish mechanisms for stakeholder engagement, such as shareholder meetings, investor relations activities, and stakeholder advisory panels. These mechanisms facilitate communication, feedback, and input from stakeholders, enabling organizations to consider their interests and concerns in decision-making processes.

By adhering to the key principles and implementing the framework components outlined in the OECD Principles of Corporate Governance, organizations can establish a strong foundation for effective governance, promote transparency and accountability, and build trust with stakeholders.

17.3 Integrating OECD Principles of Corporate Governance with Other Governance Standards and Practices

he OECD Principles of Corporate Governance can be integrated with other governance standards and practices to create a comprehensive governance framework. For example, they can be aligned with ISO 38500 for corporate governance of IT, COSO

Framework for internal control, or IIA Standards for internal auditing and governance processes. Integration of the OECD Principles with other standards allows organizations to leverage synergies and ensure consistency in governance practices across different domains. It enables a holistic approach to governance, where corporate governance practices are aligned with overall organizational governance objectives.

Chapter 18: COSO Framework

18.1 Overview of COSO Framework

The COSO (Committee of Sponsoring Organizations of the Treadway Commission) Framework provides guidance on internal control, risk management, and fraud prevention. It is a widely recognized framework that helps organizations establish effective systems for managing risks, ensuring reliable financial reporting, and preventing fraudulent activities.

18.2 Key Principles and Framework Components

The COSO Framework is based on a set of key principles that organizations should follow when implementing internal control and risk management practices. These principles include:

- **Risk Assessment:** The principle of risk assessment focuses on the identification and assessment of risks that could impact the achievement of organizational objectives. It encourages organizations to establish a systematic process for identifying, analysing, and prioritizing risks. By understanding their risk profile, organizations can develop appropriate risk responses and mitigation strategies.

- **Control Activities:** The COSO Framework highlights the need for control activities that mitigate identified risks. Control activities include policies, procedures, and practices that are designed to ensure that organizational objectives are achieved, risks are managed effectively, and financial reporting is reliable. Control activities can be preventive, detective, or corrective in nature.

- **Information and Communication:** The principle of information and communication emphasizes the importance of relevant and reliable information for effective decision-making and internal control. Organizations should establish robust information systems and communication channels to ensure that information flows appropriately throughout the organization. This includes clear communication of objectives, roles, responsibilities, and policies.

- **Monitoring Activities:** The COSO Framework promotes ongoing monitoring of internal controls to ensure their effectiveness and timely identification of deficiencies. Monitoring activities include regular assessments, internal audits, management reviews, and evaluations of the internal control system. By monitoring internal controls, organizations can identify weaknesses, address deficiencies, and continuously improve their control environment.

Framework Components of COSO include:

- **Internal Control Components:** The framework outlines five components of internal control: Control Environment, Risk Assessment, Control Activities, Information and

Communication, and Monitoring Activities. These components collectively contribute to the establishment of effective internal control systems.

- **Internal Control Objectives:** COSO defines five internal control objectives that organizations should strive to achieve. These objectives relate to the reliability of financial reporting, effectiveness and efficiency of operations, compliance with laws and regulations, safeguarding of assets, and overall risk management.

- **Control Framework and Criteria:** The COSO Framework provides a comprehensive control framework and criteria that organizations can use to assess and evaluate the effectiveness of their internal control systems. The framework outlines the principles and attributes of effective internal control, helping organizations establish a strong control environment.

By adhering to the key principles and implementing the framework components outlined in the COSO Framework, organizations can enhance their internal control systems, manage risks effectively, and ensure reliable financial reporting.

18.3 Integrating COSO Framework with Other Governance Standards and Practices

The COSO Framework can be integrated with other governance standards and practices to create a comprehensive governance framework. For example, it can be aligned with COBIT for IT governance and management, ISO 31000 for risk management, or IIA Standards for internal auditing and governance processes.

Integration of the COSO Framework with other standards allows organizations to leverage synergies and ensure consistency in governance practices across different domains. It enables a holistic approach to governance, where internal control and risk management practices are aligned with overall organizational governance objectives.

Chapter 19: IIA Standards

19.1 Overview of IIA Standards

The IIA (Institute of Internal Auditors) Standards provide guidance for internal auditing, risk management, and governance processes. They are internationally recognized standards that help organizations establish effective internal audit functions, assess risks, and ensure compliance with laws, regulations, and internal policies.

18.2 Key Principles and Framework Components

The IIA Standards are based on a set of key principles that organizations should follow when implementing internal auditing and governance practices. These principles include:

- **Integrity:** The IIA emphasizes the importance of integrity in internal auditing activities. Internal auditors should be honest, ethical, and impartial in carrying out their responsibilities. They should adhere to professional standards and exercise due care in their work.

- **Objectivity:** The principle of objectivity emphasizes the need for internal auditors to maintain an unbiased and impartial approach in their evaluations and assessments. They should remain independent and avoid conflicts of interest that could compromise their objectivity.

- **Confidentiality:** The IIA recognizes the importance of confidentiality in internal auditing. Internal auditors should exercise discretion and protect the confidentiality of information obtained during their work. They should only disclose information on a need-to-know basis and in accordance with applicable laws and regulations.

- **Competence:** The principle of competence highlights the need for internal auditors to possess the knowledge, skills, and experience necessary to perform their roles effectively. They should continually enhance their professional competence through training, education, and ongoing professional development.

Framework Components of IIA Standards include:

- **Attribute Standards:** The IIA Standards define a set of attribute standards that internal auditors should possess and maintain. These standards cover areas such as independence, objectivity, competence, confidentiality, and professional behaviour. Attribute standards ensure that internal auditors have the necessary qualities to perform their roles effectively.

- **Performance Standards:** The IIA Standards provide performance standards that guide the conduct of internal audit engagements. These standards outline the responsibilities and activities that internal auditors should undertake during the various phases of an audit, including planning, fieldwork, and reporting. Performance standards ensure that internal audits are conducted in a systematic and effective manner.

- **Implementation Standards:** The IIA Standards also include implementation standards that address specific areas of internal auditing, such as governance, risk management, and control processes. These standards provide additional guidance on how internal auditors can fulfill their responsibilities in these areas.

By adhering to the key principles and implementing the framework components outlined in the IIA Standards, organizations can establish effective internal audit functions, enhance risk management practices, and ensure compliance with governance requirements.

19.3 Integrating IIA Standards with Other Governance Standards and Practices

The IIA Standards can be integrated with other governance standards and practices to create a comprehensive governance framework. For example, they can be aligned with COBIT for IT governance and management, COSO Framework for internal control, or ISO 31000 for risk management. Integration of the IIA Standards with other standards allows organizations to leverage synergies and ensure consistency in governance practices across different domains. It enables a holistic approach to governance, where internal auditing and governance processes are aligned with overall organizational governance objectives.

Chapter 20: NIST Cybersecurity Framework

20.1 Overview of NIST Cybersecurity Framework

The NIST (National Institute of Standards and Technology) Cybersecurity Framework provides guidelines and best practices for managing and mitigating cybersecurity risks. It is a voluntary framework that helps organizations identify, protect, detect, respond to, and recover from cybersecurity incidents. The framework promotes a proactive and risk-based approach to cybersecurity, enabling organizations to strengthen their cybersecurity posture.

20.2 Key Principles and Framework Components

The NIST Cybersecurity Framework is based on a set of key principles that organizations should follow when implementing cybersecurity practices. These principles include:

- **Identify:** The principle of identify focuses on understanding and managing cybersecurity risks. Organizations should identify their critical assets, assess vulnerabilities, and determine the potential impact of cybersecurity incidents. By identifying risks, organizations can prioritize their cybersecurity efforts and allocate resources effectively.

- **Protect:** The principle of protect emphasizes the need for protective measures to prevent or mitigate cybersecurity threats. Organizations should implement safeguards, such as access controls, encryption, and secure configurations, to protect their systems, networks, and data from unauthorized access or damage.

- **Detect:** The principle of detect focuses on the timely detection of cybersecurity incidents. Organizations should implement monitoring systems, intrusion detection mechanisms, and security event management processes to identify and respond to cybersecurity events promptly. Early detection enables organizations to minimize the impact of incidents and initiate effective response measures.

- **Respond:** The principle of respond emphasizes the need for a well-defined response plan to address cybersecurity incidents. Organizations should establish an incident response capability, including communication protocols, incident reporting mechanisms, and predefined procedures. A timely and coordinated response helps organizations contain and mitigate the impact of cybersecurity incidents.

- **Recover:** The principle of recover focuses on restoring normal operations after a cybersecurity incident. Organizations should develop recovery plans and procedures to restore systems, networks, and data to a secure and functional state. The recovery process includes evaluating lessons learned, implementing improvements, and restoring confidence in the organization's cybersecurity resilience.

Framework Components of NIST Cybersecurity Framework include:

- **Core Functions:** The framework defines five core functions that represent the key activities involved in managing cybersecurity risks. These functions are Identify, Protect, Detect, Respond, and Recover. Each core function is associated with specific categories and subcategories that provide detailed guidance on cybersecurity practices.

- **Implementation Tiers:** The NIST Cybersecurity Framework also introduces implementation tiers that reflect the maturity of an organization's cybersecurity practices. The tiers range from Partial (Tier 1) to Adaptive (Tier 4). Organizations can assess their current cybersecurity posture and determine the desired tier to target for improvement.

By adhering to the key principles and implementing the framework components outlined in the NIST Cybersecurity Framework, organizations can enhance their cybersecurity resilience, protect critical assets, and effectively manage cybersecurity risks.

20.3 Integrating NIST Cybersecurity Framework with Other Governance Standards and Practices

The NIST Cybersecurity Framework can be integrated with other governance standards and practices to create a comprehensive governance framework. For example, it can be aligned with COBIT for IT governance and management, ISO 27001 for information security management, or COSO Framework for internal control. Integration of the NIST Cybersecurity Framework with other standards allows organizations to leverage synergies and ensure consistency in governance practices across different domains. It enables a holistic approach to governance, where cybersecurity practices are aligned with overall organizational governance objectives.

Chapter 21: King IV Report

21.1 Overview of King IV Report

The King IV Report provides principles and practices for effective governance, with an emphasis on ethical leadership, stakeholder inclusivity, and integrated reporting. It is a governance framework specifically designed for South African organizations, promoting responsible and sustainable business practices.

21.2 Key Principles and Framework Components

The King IV Report is based on a set of key principles that organizations should follow when implementing governance practices. These principles include:

- **Ethical and Effective Leadership:** The King IV Report emphasizes the importance of ethical and effective leadership in driving good governance. Organizations should establish a culture of integrity, promote ethical behaviour, and demonstrate leadership commitment to responsible governance practices.

- **Corporate Citizenship and Stakeholder Inclusivity:** The principle of corporate citizenship focuses on the organization's responsibility to consider and respond to the needs and interests of its stakeholders. Organizations should engage with stakeholders, establish effective communication channels, and ensure that their decisions and actions consider the broader social and environmental impacts.

- **Integrated Thinking and Reporting:** The King IV Report encourages organizations to adopt integrated thinking and reporting practices. Integrated thinking involves considering the organization's financial, social, and environmental performance holistically. Integrated reporting aims to provide a comprehensive view of the organization's value creation, considering financial, social, and environmental aspects.

- **Risk Management and Internal Control:** The principle of risk management and internal control promotes the establishment of effective systems to identify, assess, and manage risks. Organizations should implement robust risk management processes and establish internal control systems that provide reasonable assurance regarding the achievement of objectives.

Framework Components of the King IV Report include:

- **Principles and Practices:** The framework outlines a set of principles and practices that organizations should adopt to achieve effective governance. These principles cover areas such as leadership, ethics, risk management, governance structures, remuneration, and reporting. The practices provide guidance on how to implement and apply the principles effectively.

- **Apply or Explain Approach:** The King IV Report promotes an apply or explain approach, where organizations should either apply the recommended practices or explain why alternative practices are more suitable. This approach encourages transparency and accountability in governance practices.

By adhering to the key principles and implementing the framework components outlined in the King IV Report, South African organizations can establish a foundation for responsible and sustainable governance, promote stakeholder inclusivity, and enhance transparency in reporting.

21.3 Integrating King IV Report with Other Governance Standards and Practices

The King IV Report can be integrated with other governance standards and practices to create a comprehensive governance framework. For example, it can be aligned with the OECD Principles of Corporate Governance, ISO 26000 for social responsibility, or GRI Standards for sustainability reporting. Integration of the King IV Report with other standards allows organizations to leverage synergies and ensure consistency in governance practices across different domains. It enables a holistic approach to governance, where governance practices are aligned with overall organizational governance objectives.

Chapter 22: Integrating Multiple Governance Standards and Frameworks

22.1 Establishing an Integrated Governance Framework

In today's complex business environment, organizations often need to comply with multiple governance standards and frameworks. Integrating these standards and frameworks into a cohesive governance framework helps organizations streamline their governance practices, avoid duplication of efforts, and ensure alignment across different areas of governance.

To establish an integrated governance framework, organizations can follow these steps:

- **Identify relevant governance standards and frameworks:** Identify the key governance standards and frameworks that are applicable to your organization based on industry, regulatory requirements, and organizational objectives. Examples include ISO 38500 (IT governance), ISO 31000 (risk management), ISO 9001 (quality management), ISO 23635 (distributed ledger technology governance), ISO 37301 (compliance management systems), ISO 37000 (organization change management), COBIT 2019 (IT governance and management), CMMI (capability maturity model integration), and ISO 45001 (occupational health and safety management).

- **Assess commonalities and overlaps:** Analyse the identified governance standards and frameworks to identify common principles, processes, and objectives. For example, both ISO 38500 and COBIT 2019 emphasize the need for clear governance structures and decision-making processes in managing IT. Identifying these commonalities allows for a more streamlined and cohesive approach to governance.

- **Define governance objectives and priorities:** Define your organization's governance objectives and prioritize them based on their strategic importance and impact on organizational performance. For example, if the organization is in a highly regulated industry, compliance with regulatory requirements may be a top priority, while risk management and data privacy could be other important objectives.

- **Map and align governance practices:** Map the requirements, processes, and controls from each governance standard and framework to identify commonalities and areas of alignment. For example, ISO 9001 and ISO 45001 both emphasize the importance of establishing objectives, conducting internal audits, and implementing corrective actions. Mapping these practices helps identify areas of overlap and synergies that can be leveraged for integration.

- **Develop an integrated governance framework:** Based on the mapping and alignment exercise, develop an integrated governance framework that brings together the relevant practices from different standards and frameworks. For example, the organization could develop a governance framework that includes risk management practices from ISO 31000, compliance management practices from ISO 37301, and IT governance practices from COBIT 2019. This framework should reflect the organization's unique context, goals, and compliance requirements.

- **Communicate and train:** Communicate the integrated governance framework to all stakeholders, including senior management, employees, and external partners. Provide training and awareness sessions to ensure that everyone understands the framework, their roles, and the benefits of integration. For example, conducting training sessions on the integrated governance framework can help employees understand how different governance practices work together and how their work aligns with organizational goals.

- **Monitor and review:** Regularly monitor and review the effectiveness of the integrated governance framework. Collect feedback from stakeholders, assess the framework's impact on organizational performance, and make necessary adjustments to improve its efficiency and effectiveness. For example, conducting periodic reviews and audits can help identify areas for improvement and ensure that the integrated governance framework continues to meet the organization's evolving needs.

By establishing an integrated governance framework, organizations can streamline their governance practices, reduce duplication of efforts, and create a unified approach to governance that aligns with organizational goals and objectives. Integrating governance standards and frameworks enables organizations to leverage synergies, optimize resources, and effectively address the diverse requirements of different governance areas.

Chapter 23: Key Stakeholders in Governance

23.1 Identifying and Understanding Key Stakeholders

Stakeholders play a crucial role in governance as they have a vested interest in the organization and its operations. Identifying and understanding key stakeholders is essential for effective governance. Stakeholders can be categorized into internal and external stakeholders.

Internal stakeholders typically include:

- **Board of Directors:** The board of directors consists of individuals elected or appointed to represent the shareholders' interests. They have the ultimate responsibility for the organization's strategic direction, decision-making, and oversight. The board sets governance policies, monitors organizational performance, and ensures compliance with legal and regulatory requirements.

- **Senior Management:** Senior executives, such as the CEO, CFO, and COO, are responsible for implementing the board's decisions and managing the day-to-day operations of the organization. They provide leadership, develop, and execute strategies, allocate resources, and ensure that governance policies and practices are followed throughout the organization.

- **Employees:** Employees are key stakeholders who contribute to the organization's success and are directly impacted by governance decisions. They play a vital role in ensuring compliance with policies and procedures, reporting concerns or violations, and actively participating in training and awareness programs. Engaging employees in governance processes can enhance their commitment and foster a culture of accountability and ethical behaviour.

- **Shareholders:** Shareholders are individuals or entities that hold ownership shares in the organization. They have a financial interest in the organization's performance and governance practices. Shareholders exercise their rights through voting on significant matters, such as the appointment of directors, changes to the organization's articles of incorporation, or major business decisions. Engaging shareholders and providing transparency in governance practices can build trust and strengthen the organization's relationship with its owners.

External stakeholders typically include:

- **Customers:** Customers are essential stakeholders whose satisfaction and trust are crucial for the organization's success. Governance practices should prioritize customer interests, such as providing quality products or services, ensuring data privacy and security, and resolving customer complaints promptly and fairly. Engaging with customers and seeking their feedback can help organizations better understand their needs and expectations.

- **Suppliers and Business Partners:** Suppliers and business partners contribute to the organization's value chain and play a significant role in its success. Effective governance involves establishing mutually beneficial relationships, ensuring fair practices, and managing risks associated with supplier and partner engagements. Organizations should consider factors such as supplier diversity, responsible sourcing, and supply chain transparency in their governance practices.

- **Regulatory Authorities:** Regulatory authorities establish laws and regulations that organizations must comply with. They oversee compliance with governance standards and may conduct audits or investigations to ensure adherence to legal requirements. Organizations must understand and meet their obligations to regulatory authorities to maintain good standing, avoid penalties, and mitigate legal risks.

- **Communities and Society:** Organizations have a responsibility to the communities and societies in which they operate. Governance practices should consider the impact on social, environmental, and ethical factors to maintain positive relationships and contribute to sustainable development. This includes managing environmental impacts, supporting community initiatives, promoting diversity and inclusion, and ensuring ethical business practices.

23.2 Roles and Responsibilities of Stakeholders in Governance

Each stakeholder group has unique roles and responsibilities in governance:

- **Board of Directors:** The board of directors provides strategic guidance, sets policies, and ensures compliance with laws and regulations. They oversee executive management, monitor organizational performance, and make decisions in the best interest of the organization and its stakeholders. The board is responsible for establishing the governance framework, approving major strategic initiatives, and providing oversight to mitigate risks.

- **Senior Management:** Senior management is responsible for executing the board's decisions, managing day-to-day operations, and implementing governance policies and practices. They translate the organization's strategic goals into actionable plans, allocate resources, and monitor progress. Senior management plays a key role in fostering a culture of ethics, integrity, and accountability throughout the organization.

- **Employees:** Employees contribute to governance by following established policies and procedures, reporting concerns or violations, and actively participating in training and awareness programs. They are responsible for upholding ethical standards, adhering to governance guidelines, and promoting a culture of integrity and accountability. Employees should be encouraged to report any violations or risks they encounter and play an active role in improving governance practices.

- **Shareholders:** Shareholders exercise their rights by voting on key decisions and participating in annual general meetings. They have the power to hold the board accountable and influence governance practices through their ownership and engagement. Shareholders should actively engage with the organization, review disclosures and reports, and exercise their voting rights to ensure governance practices align with their expectations and protect their interests.

- **Customers:** Customers influence governance through their choices and feedback. Their satisfaction and loyalty are indicators of effective governance practices. Organizations should prioritize customer interests, provide quality products or services, ensure data privacy and security, and respond to customer concerns. Customer feedback should be actively sought and used to improve governance practices and enhance customer satisfaction.

- **Suppliers and Business Partners:** Suppliers and business partners contribute to governance by adhering to contractual obligations, ensuring quality and safety standards, and collaborating in a transparent and ethical manner. They can also provide valuable input and expertise to help organizations improve their governance practices. Building strong relationships based on trust, fairness, and shared values is essential for effective governance in supplier and partner engagements.

- **Regulatory Authorities:** Regulatory authorities establish legal and regulatory frameworks to ensure compliance and protect the interests of stakeholders. Organizations must understand

and meet their obligations to regulatory authorities. They should maintain open lines of communication, stay informed about regulatory changes, and promptly address any compliance gaps or issues. Cooperation and transparency with regulatory authorities are critical for maintaining regulatory compliance and avoiding legal risks.

- **Communities and Society:** Organizations have a social responsibility to communities and society. They should engage with stakeholders, address social and environmental concerns, and contribute to sustainable development. This includes managing environmental impacts, supporting community initiatives, promoting diversity and inclusion, and adhering to ethical business practices. Organizations should actively participate in dialogue with communities, be responsive to their needs, and demonstrate good corporate citizenship.

By understanding the roles and responsibilities of key stakeholders, organizations can effectively engage and collaborate with them in governance processes, ensuring a holistic and inclusive approach to governance.

23.3 Effective Communication and Engagement Strategies

Effective communication and engagement strategies are vital for stakeholders to understand and participate in governance processes. Key strategies include:

- **Transparency:** Organizations should strive to be transparent in their governance practices by providing clear and accessible information to stakeholders. This includes disclosing relevant financial and non-financial information, communicating risks and opportunities, and sharing progress towards goals and targets.

- **Regular Communication:** Establishing regular channels of communication, such as board meetings, management updates, employee forums, and shareholder communications, helps ensure that stakeholders are informed about governance matters and can provide input and ask questions.

- **Engagement and Consultation:** Actively engaging stakeholders in governance processes can enhance decision-making and promote a sense of ownership. This can be done through consultations, surveys, focus groups, and stakeholder forums. Organizations should provide opportunities for stakeholders to express their views and incorporate their feedback into governance practices.

- **Training and Education:** Providing training and education on governance principles, policies, and practices helps stakeholders understand their roles and responsibilities. This includes board training, employee training on ethical conduct and compliance, and shareholder education on governance processes and rights.

- **Feedback Mechanisms:** Establishing feedback mechanisms, such as whistleblower hotlines, suggestion boxes, or online platforms, allows stakeholders to report concerns, provide feedback, or seek clarification on governance matters. Organizations should ensure that these mechanisms are confidential, accessible, and responsive.

- **Stakeholder Representation:** Where appropriate, organizations may consider appointing stakeholder representatives to the board or establishing advisory committees to ensure diverse perspectives and stakeholder interests are considered in governance decision-making.

23.4 Meeting Stakeholder Expectations through Governance Practices

Meeting stakeholder expectations is critical for building trust, maintaining credibility, and achieving sustainable success. Governance practices should consider the following to meet stakeholder expectations:

- **Accountability and Transparency:** Organizations should establish robust accountability mechanisms and be transparent in their decision-making processes. This includes disclosing relevant information, reporting on progress and performance, and explaining the rationale behind decisions.

- **Ethical Conduct:** Organizations should uphold high ethical standards and promote a culture of integrity. This includes adhering to ethical codes of conduct, avoiding conflicts of interest, and addressing unethical behaviour promptly and appropriately.

- **Risk Management:** Effective risk management practices demonstrate a commitment to protecting stakeholders' interests. Organizations should identify and assess risks, implement appropriate controls, and regularly monitor and mitigate risks that could impact stakeholders.

- **Compliance with Laws and Regulations:** Organizations must comply with applicable laws, regulations, and governance standards. This includes understanding legal requirements, establishing compliance frameworks, conducting regular audits, and addressing any non-compliance issues.

- **Stakeholder Engagement:** Actively engaging stakeholders in governance processes and decision-making demonstrates respect for their input and interests. Organizations should create opportunities for meaningful engagement, consider stakeholder feedback, and communicate how stakeholder input has influenced governance decisions.

- **Performance and Quality Management:** Establishing performance and quality management systems helps organizations deliver value to stakeholders. This includes setting clear performance targets, measuring and monitoring performance, and implementing continuous improvement initiatives.

- **Sustainable Practices:** Organizations should integrate environmental, social, and governance (ESG) considerations into their governance practices. This includes managing environmental impacts, supporting social initiatives, promoting diversity and inclusion, and considering long-term sustainability in decision-making.

By understanding and meeting stakeholder expectations through effective governance practices, organizations can build trust, enhance reputation, and create long-term value for all stakeholders involved.

Chapter 24: Global Regulatory Governance Related Requirements (Examples)

24.1 Meeting Regulatory Driven Requirements

Many of the global regulators have set expectations in the form of standards or requirements they have set that organizations must demonstrate they can meet. The standards discussed within this guide can be leveraged to ensure compliance with each of these regulations. The following are examples of some of the most common regulatory body requirements.

24.1.1 US Federal Reserve Bank – Supervisory Rating

The US Federal Reserve conducts supervisory assessments of banks and assigns ratings based on various factors, including risk management, governance, and controls. These ratings help determine the level of regulatory oversight and compliance expectations. To improve their rating, organizations can focus on the following:

- **Risk Management:**
    - Implement comprehensive risk management frameworks aligned with industry best practices.
    - Establish robust risk identification, measurement, and mitigation processes.
    - Enhance risk governance through clear roles, responsibilities, and reporting structures.
    - Regularly assess and update risk appetite and tolerance levels.
    - Conduct stress testing and scenario analysis to evaluate potential risks.

- **Governance and Controls:**
    - Enhance board oversight and ensure independence and expertise among board members.
    - Implement effective internal controls to mitigate operational and compliance risks.
    - Strengthen audit and compliance functions to ensure regulatory adherence.
    - Foster a strong risk culture throughout the organization with appropriate training and incentives.
    - Implement effective internal and external audit processes.

24.1.2 Basel Committee – Basel III Banking Supervision

Basel III is an international regulatory framework developed by the Basel Committee on Banking Supervision. It aims to strengthen banks' capital adequacy, liquidity, and risk management practices. To comply with Basel III requirements, organizations must consider the following:

- **Capital Adequacy:**
    - Maintain a minimum capital requirement based on risk-weighted assets.
    - Enhance the quality and quantity of capital to absorb potential losses.
    - Implement measures to ensure capital buffers and capital conservation.

- **Liquidity Risk Management:**
    - Develop a robust liquidity risk management framework.
    - Establish liquidity risk measurement, monitoring, and reporting processes.

- o Maintain sufficient liquidity buffers to withstand stress scenarios.
- o Comply with liquidity coverage ratio (LCR) and net stable funding ratio (NSFR) requirements.

- **Risk Management and Governance:**
  - o Implement effective risk management practices across the organization.
  - o Establish comprehensive risk identification, measurement, and mitigation processes.
  - o Strengthen risk governance through clear roles, responsibilities, and reporting lines.
  - o Enhance risk culture and ensure accountability at all levels.

- **Reporting and Disclosure:**
  - o Provide transparent and accurate reporting of risk exposures and capital adequacy.
  - o Comply with reporting requirements related to capital, liquidity, and risk management.
  - o Ensure timely and comprehensive disclosure of relevant information to stakeholders.

To ensure compliance with Basel III, organizations should conduct regular self-assessments, internal audits, and stress tests. They should also establish internal controls and checks to monitor compliance with capital, liquidity, and risk management requirements. This may include automated systems, risk analytics, and reporting tools to ensure accurate measurement and reporting of risk-related information.

24.1.3 Country Specific Regulatory Requirement Standards

United Kingdom

Compliance Requirements - Companies operating in the UK need to comply with the Companies Act, which sets out legal obligations related to governance, financial reporting, and disclosure requirements.

Regulatory Standards- Organizations should follow the UK Corporate Governance Code issued by the Financial Reporting Council (FRC). It provides recommendations for corporate governance practices. For example, organizations are expected to have a balanced board, ensure board independence, establish effective risk management processes, and enhance shareholder rights. Compliance with this code includes conducting regular board evaluations, providing transparent financial reporting, and engaging with stakeholders.

United States

Compliance Requirements - Organizations in the US need to comply with various regulations depending on their industry and activities. Publicly traded companies need to comply with the Securities Exchange Act of 1934, which includes requirements for financial reporting, disclosure, and governance practices.

Regulatory Standards- Organizations should adhere to regulatory standards set by bodies such as the Securities and Exchange Commission (SEC). For example, organizations need to establish an independent board of directors, maintain accurate and transparent financial records, and disclose material information to investors. Compliance with SEC regulations includes filing periodic reports, disclosing executive compensation, and ensuring board oversight of risk management.

Canada

Compliance Requirements - Organizations in Canada need to comply with the Canada Business Corporations Act (CBCA) or provincial corporation acts, depending on their jurisdiction. These acts outline legal requirements for corporate governance, shareholder rights, disclosure, and financial reporting.

Regulatory Standards - While there are no specific local governance-related standards for each global standard listed in your book, organizations can follow guidelines provided by regulatory bodies such as the Canadian Securities Administrators (CSA). For instance, organizations should have independent board members, establish audit committees, ensure accurate financial reporting, and enhance shareholder communication. Compliance includes filing financial statements, providing timely disclosures, and holding annual general meetings.

Germany

Compliance Requirements - Organizations in Germany need to comply with the German Stock Corporation Act (AktG) and other regulations that govern corporate governance practices, financial reporting, and disclosure requirements.

Regulatory Standards - Organizations can follow recommendations provided by the German Corporate

Governance Code (DCGK). This code emphasizes principles such as board independence, transparency, and shareholder rights. Compliance includes establishing an effective supervisory board, ensuring accurate financial reporting, disclosing relevant information to shareholders, and implementing effective risk management processes.

India

Compliance Requirements - Organizations in India need to comply with the Companies Act, which outlines legal requirements for corporate governance, financial reporting, disclosure, and compliance for companies operating in the country.

Regulatory Standards - Organizations should follow regulations and guidelines issued by the Securities and Exchange Board of India (SEBI). These include maintaining board independence, establishing audit committees, enhancing financial disclosures, and engaging with shareholders. Compliance involves filing financial statements, conducting annual general meetings, ensuring board effectiveness, and implementing effective risk management practices.

Chapter 25: Summary and Conclusion

Throughout this guide, we have examined the multifaceted aspects of governance, compliance, and corporate responsibility. We started by understanding the definition and evolution of governance, its role in organizational success, and the key principles and objectives it encompasses. We explored the applicability of governance practices for organizations of all sizes and highlighted the importance of tailoring governance approaches to suit different needs.

Next, we delved into the consequences of poor governance, including its impact on business performance, legal and regulatory compliance, reputation, and finances. It became evident that effective governance is crucial for organizations to thrive and maintain their competitive edge in today's complex and fast-paced business environment.

We then dived into several prominent governance standards and frameworks. The ISO 38500 standard for corporate governance of IT provides valuable guidance for organizations in managing their IT-related risks and aligning IT with business objectives. The ISO 31000 standard for risk management offers a comprehensive framework to identify, assess, and mitigate risks. ISO 9001 for quality management focuses on ensuring consistent quality and customer satisfaction. ISO 23635 addresses governance considerations for blockchain and distributed ledger technologies. ISO 37301 provides guidance on establishing effective compliance management systems. ISO 37000 emphasizes the importance of change management in governance. COBIT 2019 offers a framework specifically designed for IT governance and management. And CMMI provides a maturity model for process improvement and governance.

We also discussed the importance of integrating governance standards and frameworks to establish a cohesive and synergistic governance approach. By mapping and aligning different governance practices, organizations can optimize their effectiveness and ensure comprehensive coverage across various domains.

Moreover, we examined the role of stakeholders in governance and highlighted the significance of stakeholder engagement, communication, and representation. Understanding the expectations and interests of stakeholders is vital for building trust, maintaining transparency, and achieving organizational objectives.

Lastly, we explored how organizations can meet stakeholder expectations through effective governance practices. This includes establishing accountability mechanisms, promoting ethical conduct, managing risks, ensuring compliance with laws and regulations, engaging stakeholders, and implementing performance and quality management systems. By embracing sustainable practices and considering environmental, social, and governance factors, organizations can demonstrate their commitment to long-term value creation.

In conclusion, effective governance is a cornerstone of organizational success, ensuring responsible decision-making, risk mitigation, and stakeholder trust. By understanding and implementing the principles, standards, and practices discussed in this guide, organizations can enhance their governance capabilities, achieve compliance, and drive sustainable growth. Remember, governance is an ongoing journey that requires continuous improvement and adaptation to changing circumstances.

I hope that the insights and knowledge shared here serve as a valuable resource for those striving to establish and maintain effective governance practices. By leveraging these principles and standards, organizations can navigate the complexities of governance, foster a culture of accountability and transparency, and position themselves for long-term success.

References

- **ISO 38500: Corporate Governance of IT -**
  https://www.iso.org/standard/38500.html

- **ISO 31000: Risk Management -**
  https://www.iso.org/standard/65694.html

- **ISO 9001: Quality Management -**
  https://www.iso.org/standard/62085.html

- **ISO 23635: Distributed Ledger Technology Governance -**
  https://www.iso.org/standard/77945.html)
- **ISO 37301: Compliance Management Systems -**
  https://www.iso.org/standard/78770.html

- **ISO 37000: Organization Change Management -**
  https://www.iso.org/standard/78616.html

- **ISO 27001: Information Security Management Systems -**
  https://www.iso.org/standard/27001

- **COBIT 2019: IT Governance and Management -**
  https://www.isaca.org/resources/cobit

- **CMMI: Capability Maturity Model Integration -**
  https://cmmiinstitute.com/cmmi

- **OECD Principles of Corporate Governance -**
  http://www.oecd.org/corporate/principles-corporate-governance/ (Reference: OECD. (2015). OECD Principles of Corporate Governance. Retrieved from http://www.oecd.org/corporate/principles-corporate-governance/)

- **COSO Framework** - https://www.coso.org/Pages/default.aspx (Reference: COSO. (2013). Internal Control - Integrated Framework. Retrieved from https://www.coso.org/Pages/ic.aspx)

- **IIA Standards** - https://na.theiia.org/Pages/IIAHome.aspx (Reference: The Institute of Internal Auditors (IIA). (2017). International Professional Practices Framework (IPPF). Retrieved from https://na.theiia.org/standards-guidance/ippf/Pages/Standards-and-Guidance-IPPF.aspx)

- **NIST Cybersecurity Framework** - https://www.nist.gov/cyberframework (Reference: NIST. (2018). Framework for Improving Critical Infrastructure Cybersecurity. Retrieved from https://www.nist.gov/cyberframework)

- **King IV Report** - https://www.iodsa.co.za/ (Reference: Institute of Directors in Southern Africa. (2016). King IV Report on Corporate Governance for South Africa. Retrieved from https://www.iodsa.co.za/page/kingivinfo)

For more practical advice and guidance on Governance Solutions Worldwide for your organization, please contact **Governance Solutions Australia** @

https://www.govaus.com.au

Streamlined Solutions, Governance Excellence